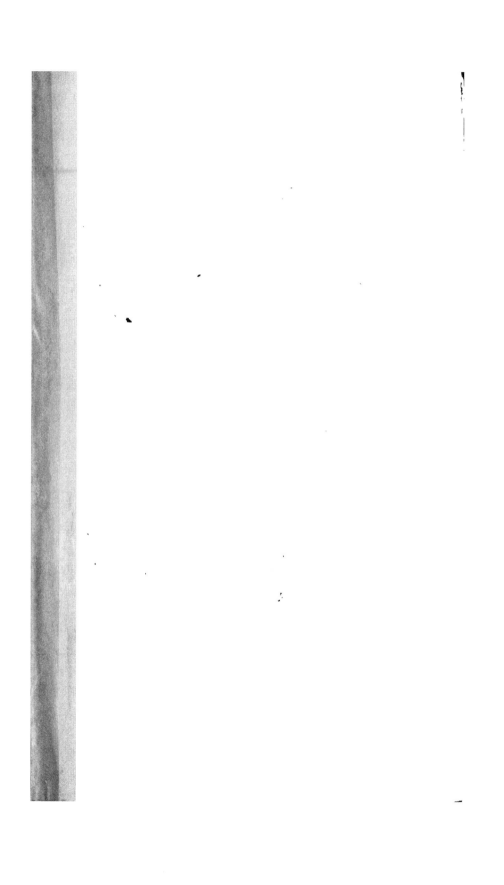

REMAINS

OF THE LATE

REV. HENRY FRANCIS LYTE, M.A.

LONDON :
GILBERT & RIVINGTON, PRINTERS,
ST. JOHN'S SQUARE.

REMAINS

OF THE LATE

REV. HENRY FRANCIS LYTE, M.A.

INCUMBENT OF LOWER BRIXHAM, DEVON;

WITH A

PREFATORY MEMOIR

BY THE EDITOR.

LONDON:

FRANCIS & JOHN RIVINGTON,

ST. PAUL'S CHURCH YARD, AND WATERLOO PLACE.

1850.

IN

Loving Memory

OF A

DEVOTED FATHER AND DEAR COMPANION,

ARE

THESE BRIEF RECORDS

GIVEN.

CONTENTS.

CONTENTS.

PREFATORY MEMOIR.

To usher into the world a quiet volume of Poetry, composed in the hours of relaxation from parochial labour, or under the chastening influence of lengthened illness, seems scarcely to harmonize with the stirring anxieties and excitement of the present time. Yet to those friends who will receive these "Remains" as a tribute of affection to the memory of one whom they dearly and deservedly loved, it is hoped their publication will not be unwelcome. It is felt, however, that much apology is due for the delay in their appearance, which, from sad and unavoidable circumstances, has occurred, as well as for the actual contents of the volume itself. It had been contemplated by the Author to present another volume of Poetry to the public, and with this view he had partially corrected and prepared for the press most of the

a

succeeding Poems.   Death, however, cut short the
work, and the unfinished MS. passed into the
hands of his second son, who inherited much of
his father's taste for literature, and would have
ably carried out the design, had he not been very
shortly summoned to follow his father into the
world unseen.   Other causes of delay, which need
not be particularized, have arisen, and the work
itself is now published in a somewhat different
form from that which had been originally intended.
Indeed the title of "Remains" may seem scarcely
suitable to a volume, which consists merely of
poems and sermons, without any other selection
from the large mass of MSS. found among the
author's papers.   On examining these papers, however, it was found that so wide and varied was the
range of notes and observations comprised in them,
and so imperfect, in many instances, the form in
which they had been left on record, that to have
given sufficient to do justice to the writer, would
have increased too greatly the bulk of the present
volume, and to have selected a few desultory re-
marks would have failed to satisfy the reader, or
faithfully to pourtray the distinctive characteristics
of their writer.   It would seem indeed that the
peculiar features which rendered him so welcome
a friend, and so prized a companion, though such

as will dwell long and fondly in the memories of those who knew him, were not best fitted to furnish materials for publication. In his sermons too he rarely, if ever, preached precisely as he wrote, and almost all his MS. discourses consist simply of heads, notes, illustrations, and Scripture proofs, leaving the connecting and filling up of the whole to be done at the time of delivery. This made it almost impossible to select from his parochial sermons; and those who best remember his own peculiar flow of eloquence, and charm of voice and manner, will not fail, in glancing over the few sermons given in this volume, to feel how far short they fall of his own impressive and impassioned style, when wanting his voice to utter, and his mind to add its own grace and finish to the whole.

A few unpublished earlier poems are added to those before mentioned; and it is thought that some notices of the dates and circumstances under which many of the pieces were written, together with extracts from some of his private letters, may enable the editor to give such a brief sketch of his life and character, as will add interest to the volume.

HENRY FRANCIS LYTE was born at Kelso on the 1st of June, A.D. 1793, and spent his childhood under the gentle influence and teaching of a mother

whose memory through life he cherished with fond
affection. From thence, at nine years of age, he
was sent to school at Protoro, in Ireland, but
though descended from an old and highly respect-
able family, (that of Lyte of Lyte's Carey, in the
county of Somerset), and himself the son of an
officer in the army, he was left at an early age
with scarcely any other resources for education and
advancement in life than such as the kindness of
friends, or his own abilities procured for him.
Nor were these found wanting. The high order
and versatility of his talents, shown even in
boyhood, firm integrity, and winning disposition
gained for him many a friend, and enabled him to
surmount the difficulties which beset his path; and
after passing honourably through his course at school,
under the tuition, and by the aid, of the late Dean
Burrows, he entered Trinity College, Dublin, in 1812,
where he obtained a scholarship in the following
year. During his academical career he cultivated his
natural talent for poetry, and was the successful
competitor for three English prize poems, in three
successive years: one of these, " The Battle of
Salamanca," is inserted in the present volume;
together with two or three minor pieces, to which
dates are attached, as fair specimens of his poetical
attainments at this period. By carrying off, in

these and other instances, the rewards which were
liberally offered by the seniors of the university to
her junior members, and by taking private pupils,
he was enabled to add very agreeably to his limited
income; and, at the same time, his talents and
personal attractions gained for him a high position
among his contemporaries. He thus formed many
valuable friendships, which were of rare warmth,
and long duration, begun in all the fervency of .
youth, and continued, in many instances, with
scarcely less ardour, through succeeding years,
altered fortunes, and broken intercourse. The
meetings of a little band of kindred souls in
these college days is thus described by him in a
stanza of a poetical letter, dated 1812, "addressed
to my friend J. K."

"And then those nights, those Attic nights we've pass'd
   With the fond few who felt and thought as we,
   Chiding the hours that stole away so fast,
   On wings of reason, wit, and minstrelsy:
   When my young muse would list and learn from thee
   Strains she had envied any tongue but thine,
   Or from discussions fanciful and free,
   On books, men, things gay, moral, and divine,
   Glean'd much to please and mend, enlighten and refine."

* The second poem given in this volume, headed

---

* The Editor cannot resist here giving, though somewhat out
of place, the following lines, addressed by this friend to H. F. L.,

"Stanzas to J. K." was the last of a series of poetical letters which pleasantly diversified a life-long correspondence, from the first of which the above extract is taken. And to the same source

---

in 1838, to which those in the volume are a reply, feeling confident, that by their own grace and sweetness, they will commend themselves to every poetic reader:—

To H. F. L.

" Eheu! fugaces, Postume, Postume,
    Labuntur anni!"—Hor.

I.

" The blithe age of childhood
    'Tis gladsome to me,
To watch its wild gambols
    And list to its glee.
Sport on, merry elves!
    Your brief respite enjoy,
Ere the cares of the man
    Quench the smiles of the boy!
Like brilliants of dew,
    In the new-risen day,
Your joys, while they sparkle,
    Are passing away!

II.

" Alas for the changes
    That time bringeth on!
Life's morn, how soon over,
    Its manna soon gone!

we are indebted for many notices contained in
his earlier letters, of his history at the periods of
their composition. The effects, however, of his

> The heart's first affections,—
> The purest and best!
> The mind's glowing fancies,
> The laugh and the jest,
> Night's calm, downy slumbers,
> Wild rambles by day,
> Are sweets only tasted
> While passing away!

III.

> " The labours of manhood,
> It grieves me to view,
> So artful, so slavish,
> So profitless too!
> The lovers of mammon
> Still toiling for gain;
> The seekers of pleasure,
> But finders of pain!
> True flowers that fail not,
> True riches that stay,
> They forfeit—for false ones
> Still passing away!

IV.

> " Friend truest and dearest!
> My partner so long
> In joy and in sorrow,
> In study and song!

struggle at the outset of life, and the fact of being
thrown entirely on his own resources left an
abiding impress on his character. There was then
formed, and afterwards more fully developed, an
energy of purpose, and a vigorous determina-
tion to overcome all difficulties, which contrasted
strangely with his natural gentleness of disposition,
and calm enjoyment of intellectual pursuits—

In the vain strife to mingle
Like me ever loth,
Of a world that's too selfish,
Too subtle for both !
Our griefs will soon end,
For our locks are now grey ;
And how swift is life's autumn
In passing away !

v.

" But, praise to Thy bounty,
Redeemer of men !
A world yet awaits us,
Where friends meet again !
A world all so holy,
So happy and fair,
That nought which offendeth
Or paineth is there !
No cloud to its summer,
No night to its day ;
No sinning, no sighing,
No passing away !"

while his high classical attainments, which he pursued the more ardently from a keen perception of, and love for, their own beauty, imparted an almost Attic elegance of thought and diction, and gave a poetic colouring to his view of the most ordinary things of life. This he never lost, and this threw a peculiar charm over his mind, which had failed in this, our bustling age, to acquire and adopt the utilitarian tone too common around us. But, above all, his grateful sense of early benefits never passed away; and in after years he paid a happy tribute to this memory of the past by the graceful extension of a like benevolence to others whenever opportunity offered. He was also naturally gifted with that open-handed liberality and largeness of soul, which is the usual accompaniment of an impetuous and ardent spirit. He had nothing for himself, and never appeared happier than in the exercise of the most universal hospitality and unwearying generosity.

To return, however, to our narrative. On leaving college, the medical profession was that which he at first proposed to enter; and from his extensive use in after life of the knowledge which he then acquired, it would appear that he had made considerable progress in his preparation for it. Subsequently, however, he was led, under the influence

of religious conviction, to devote himself to the
more sacred calling of the Christian ministry. An
extract from a letter to the valued friend before
mentioned, will give, in his own words, a sketch of
his history at this period.

"March, 1815.

"Since I last wrote to you I have been ordained,
and have obtained a curacy within seven miles of
the town of Wexford. Here I had at first settled,
'remote from towns,' in almost perfect seclusion,
giving myself up to the duties of my situation,
writing my sermons, visiting my sick, catechizing
my children, without other companions than my
flute, my pen, and my books. This answered very
well for a little time, while I had plenty of occupation on my hands.

"However, it was too great a change from the
comfort, the society, and the carelessness which I
had before enjoyed, to be long capable of satisfying
my wishes. I found myself obliged to submit to
constant intrusions, to attend long, formal dinner-
parties, to take long rides at night, or give up the
best part of my time to my neighbours, and other
miseries which I had not taken into account, when
I had resolved upon living 'passing rich,' &c., in
seclusion. All this, with some other causes also,
determined me to attend to the solicitations of my

old friend B. to continue in my care of his boys, and in my partaking his home and society. I am now settled again with him. . . . . I believe that I mentioned to you a composition, entitled 'Richard Cœur de Lion,' which I had sent in for a Chancellor's premium in college, and which was successful. On looking over this, the Provost imagined, with his telescopic eyes, that he had discovered some merit sufficient to entitle it to recitation at the last visitation. I was therefore commanded to attend with my poem, and gave them a dose of about 200 lines from the beginning of the composition, which the Chancellor liked so well, that he wished for the rest of the work for perusal. This I, with my usual dilatoriness, have not yet sent him. However, the Provost has expressed a wish that I should publish the poem, 'dedicated to the Vice-Chancellor,' and ' at the desire of the Board and Fellows of the University '. . . I have, since my first success, obtained another first prize, for a production in blank comperian verse, upon ' The Peace,' which some of the fellows have wished me to subjoin to the former ; a request which I positively will not now comply with." . .

An extract from another letter to the same friend, after a pause in their correspondence, will be read with much interest, as detailing the circumstances which first led him to embrace far deeper and more solemn views of his new position; and from this point we may date the growth, under God's blessing, of that religious character which was to be hereafter developed in so much zeal, energy, and devotion to his Master's service.

"Marazion, March 30, 1818.

"I must now tell you by what circumstances I have been brought to this place, and into this new connexion. When I last corresponded with you, I was, I think, returned to my friend I. B. from my dreary curacy of Taghinon in Ireland. Here I lived for some time, comfortably enough, assisting him in taking care of his two sons, riding about, shooting, dancing, and attending my curacy every Sunday. From this motley round of occupations, I was, however, withdrawn, by a circumstance which led the way to all my future wanderings. A neighbouring clergyman, with whom I was intimate, and who bore the highest character for benevolence, piety, and good sense, was taken ill, and sent for me. I went to attend him, and witnessed all the workings of his mind and body for some weeks till he expired. I shall never forget some of the circumstances that took place: his serious and anxious inquiries into the evidence on which a future state *existed*, his examination into the grounds on which the Scripture stood as an authentic revelation, and his convictions that it was a just statement of that which is, and is to be, all seemed to pass before him, as he stood just on the confines of eternity, as strong and distinct realities, as the parts of a picture, rather than of an abstract speculation. These preliminaries settled, his inquiry next was, the means by which a happy eternity was to be attained—and here indeed my blood almost curdled, to hear the dying man declare and prove, with irrefutable clearness, that both he and I had been utterly mistaken in the means we had adopted for ourselves, and recommended to others, if the explanatory Epistles of St. Paul were to be taken in their plain and literal sense. You can hardly perhaps conceive the effect of all this, proceeding from such a man, in such a situation. He died, I rejoice to say, happy under the belief, that though he had deeply erred, there was ONE whose death and sufferings would atone for his delinquencies, and be accepted for all that he had incurred. I was greatly affected by the whole matter, and brought to look at life and its issue with a different eye than before; and I began to study my Bible, and preach in another manner than I had previously done.

" . . . . . I had also the care of all the concerns of my friend's widow and young family,
which I arranged for them by incessant exertion
for four months. The excessive labour of mind
and body which these concomitant circumstances
brought upon me, soon proved too much for my
constitution, already enfeebled by my attendance
on my dying friend. I fell into a rapid decline,
and was ordered immediately to leave the country
for the Continent, if I wished to live. While I
was on the Continent, I continued, with the exception of a two months' residence in Paris, in constant motion, according to the direction of my
Physician; and the exercise, air, and agreeable and
diversified scenes I passed through, soon restored
me to my accustomed state of health. . . . .

" On my return to England, after a short visit to
Bristol, I came down to this part of the kingdom,
as the most likely to agree with my constitution,
and after being jostled about from one curacy to
another, I at last settled as lecturer to this little
town."

Before proceeding with our biographical sketch,
we venture to make one more extract from his early
letters to the same friend, exemplifying the literary
tone which their correspondence often assumed.
" In the rich, the imaginative, the playful, the

tender, you are quite at home, and I trust that
your subject is one replete with topics which will
call your talents in these respects peculiarly into
play.   Moore is, I think, the author of the present
day whose style most resembles yours.   I have
read his Lalla Rookh with much delight, and
thought the strictures of the Edinburgh Reviewers
on it very just.   It is perhaps too full of beauties ;
it is a picture all lights, and no shades ; the mind
looks in vain for a resting-place in reading it.   The
ornaments are so numerous in every part, that
they distract the eye from the simple beauty of the
whole.   Perhaps the conceits too with which it
abounds, beautiful as they are, tire from their
frequency at last.   Such I know were my feelings
on reading this exquisite production.   In another
respect, too, I think Moore generally fails ; and this
is, in his attempt at the sublime.   He very frequently here mistakes words for ideas, and imagines
that when he has collected a certain number of
swelling epithets together, they must necessarily
suggest a sublime image to the reader ; but if
they do, it is a sublime image of froth.   True
sublimity is ever simple in conception and expression.   The ideas must not be complex, but unique,
and the fewer the words used to convey them, the
better.   There must be nothing strained, stalking,

or grandiloquent in that which aspires to the title of sublime." It was at Marazion, whence the above letter is dated, that our author met with, and subsequently married, Anne, only daughter of Rev. W. Maxwell, D.D., of Bath, and of Falkland in the county of Monaghan; he did not remain long in Cornwall after his marriage, but removed, on account of ill health, to the neighbourhood of Lymington. To this more congenial atmosphere, and to the fuller leisure which he enjoyed in this quiet country life, we owe a large portion of his poetical writings.

He here completed a volume entitled "Tales on the Lord's Prayer," which was not however published till the year 1826, and composed many miscellaneous poems, some of which appeared in another volume entitled, "Poems chiefly religious," which was published in 1833. Of the former work we find the following favourable notice in Blackwood's Magazine, (Noctes Ambros.) No. 165, p. 686:—

"Have you seen a little volume entitled 'Tales in Verse' by the Rev. H. F. Lyte, which seems to have reached a second edition? Now that is the right kind of religious poetry. Mr. Lyte shows how the sins and sorrows of man flow from irreligion, in simple yet strong domestic narratives, told in a

style and spirit reminding one sometimes of Gold-
smith, and sometimes of Crabbe. A volume so
humble in its appearance and pretensions runs
the risk of being jostled off the highway into bye-
paths; and indeed no harm if it should; for in
such retired places it will be pleasant reading—
pensive in the shade and cheerful in the sunshine.
Mr. Lyte has reaped

> 'The harvest of a quiet eye,
> That broods and sleeps on its own heart;'

and his Christian Tales will be read with interest
and instruction by many a fireside. 'The brothers'
is eminently beautiful.—*He ought to give us another
volume.*"

This composition, however, begun at the suggestion of a literary friend, did not satisfy its author,
who thus speaks of it in his Preface. "There are
indeed many things which the Author could wish to
see altered, some which, had time permitted, he
would gladly have expunged and rewritten altogether;" and this view of its defects was never
altered.

But his muse found a sadder theme, during his
residence in Hampshire, in the loss of an infant
daughter; and the little piece in the present
volume, entitled " Lines to A. M. M. L.," or, as
we find them headed in his own MS., " Inscription

for the grave of my dear little one, Anna Maria, who died at Sway cottage, February, 1821, aged one month," was written on this occasion.

Restored health, however, brought with it the desire for a settled sphere of active ministerial labour, and he removed to the more genial clime of South Devon, where he held, for a year or two, the curacy of Charlton, near Kingsbridge. Previously to this, he had taken a cottage at Dittisham, on the banks of the river Dart, and thence had more than once officiated at Lower Brixham. His impressions of the parish were not, however, calculated to attract the sympathy of a refined and highly cultivated mind; and it was only when various concurring circumstances appeared to point it out as his path of duty, that he overcame his reluctance to enter on so uncongenial a sphere, and consented to take charge of the new district church which had been recently erected. From its original state of a fishing village, Brixham had grown up into a district of some thousands of inhabitants, increased chiefly during the war, when Torbay was the rendezvous of the Channel fleet, and Berry Head a permanent military station. From these sources, as well as from the occupations of a fishing and seafaring life, money had been made by the shrewd and busy, but uneducated people; among whom

many of the vices consequent upon the presence of
a large body of military and naval forces had taken
root, and shed an influence most unfavourable to
the growth of morality or religion.   It was not
surprising that under these circumstances, law-
lessness, immorality, and ignorance, prevailed to a
fearful extent; and it required unwonted vigour
and devotion of heart successfully to grapple with
existing evils.   In this hitherto neglected portion
of his Lord's Vineyard our Author lived and
laboured, for a period extending over more than
twenty-five years; and though human judgment
would have assigned to his talents and inclination
a very different sphere, few who beheld the mar-
vellous change wrought, by the blessing of God, in
a few years among the sailors and fishermen of
Brixham, but would confess that unerring wisdom
was especially shown in placing him as pastor over
this rough but warm-hearted people.   It would
seem, indeed, that some of the characteristics we
have before noticed, singularly fitted him for the
useful and happy discharge of his duties here: even
his own inner life of intellectual and poetic thought,
where he breathed another atmosphere from that
which hung around his daily path, strengthened
and refreshed his spirit amid much toil and weariness, and imparted a higher tone, which insensibly

attracted and influenced persons of every class with whom he came in contact. By the earnest devotion of all his powers, and the Christian charity which, in the fullest acceptation of the word, characterized his ministry, he won the affection, and roused the sympathy of his people, and gained from them support and assistance in carrying out his various plans for the spiritual and temporal amelioration of his flock. He early set on foot the now usual, but then comparatively uncommon machinery of schools and district visiting among the poor and sick, and soon numbered in the Sunday schools between 700 and 800 children, and a body of between seventy and eighty voluntary teachers, whom he himself trained and organized, frequently meeting them in a body, when, after the routine business of the school was settled, he gave them religious instruction, with especial reference to their own teaching, and took the opportunity of touching on any points in which, individually or collectively, they needed advice or assistance; thus opening that most valuable channel of ministerial usefulness, a confidential communication on matters of faith and practice between a pastor and his people. He always spent some time also in the schools during the hours of instruction, closing one or other of them in person, and addressing a few

words' of encouragement, or pointing out any
defects which had come beneath his notice. He
was peculiarly happy in availing himself of such
occasions either to impart instruction or convey
reproof, and by the aptness of his illustrations as
well as the gentleness of his manner, he fixed the
attention, and won the affection of both teachers
and scholars. His facility in composition enabled
him to furnish his schools with hymns, and works
of elementary instruction, of which there were
comparatively few at that time suitable to their
wants. He used also, when the Annual School
Feast came round, (who that ever shared those
festive meetings, but will remember the joyous
voices, the bright faces, the happy influence shed
over all by the one loving, benevolent spirit at the
head of the little band ?) generally to present them
with one or more hymns new for the occasion, often
supplying music as well as words. Many of these
have found their way into various selections of
hymns, but we venture to subjoin one of the latest,
a great favourite among the children, and in singing
which they still delight to cherish the memory of
its beloved Author.

I.

" Hark ! round the God of Love
Angels are singing !
Saints at His feet above
Their crowns are flinging.

And may poor children dare
　Hope for acceptance there,
Their simple praise and prayer
　To His throne bringing?

ii.

" Yes! through adoring throngs
　His pity sees us,
'Midst their seraphic songs
　Our offering pleases.
And Thou, who here didst prove
　To babes so full of love,
Thou art the same above,
　Merciful Jesus!

iii.

" Not a poor sparrow falls
　But Thou art near it.
When the young raven calls,
　Thou, Lord, dost hear it.
Flowers, worms, and insects share,
　Hourly Thy guardian care—
Wilt Thou bid us despair?—
　Lord, can we fear it?

iv.

" Lord, then Thy mercy send
　On all before Thee!
Children and children's friend,
　Bless, we implore Thee!
Lead us from grace to grace,
　On through our earthly race,
Till all before Thy face
　Meet to adore Thee!"

He also ventured to attempt what so many of our Christian poets have, with various success, endeavoured to produce,—a Metrical Version of the Psalms. Not, indeed, (as he tells us in his elegant little preface,) that he flattered himself with the idea of being fully able to supply that which so many have tried in vain to furnish; but that, by somewhat modifying the object aimed at, and adding to his own compositions the best and most popular passages of the ordinary new version of our Church, he might possibly frame a substitute for what he, in common with most Churchmen, earnestly wished to see: "An appropriate manual of Psalmody, provided by the heads of the Established Church, and stamped with authority for general use." The difference between his own and previous works of this kind was, that "instead of attempting a new version of the Psalms," he "simply endeavoured to give the *spirit* of each Psalm in such a compass as the public taste would tolerate, and to furnish, sometimes, when the length of the original would admit of it, an almost literal translation, sometimes, a kind of spiritual paraphrase, and at others even a brief commentary on the whole Psalm." We have some proof that this little work fulfilled its Author's design, in the fact of its adoption as a whole in some congregations of our own and the sister Church of America, and the frequent use of portions of it in most modern selections of Psalmody. Its title, also, the "Spirit of the Psalms," would seem to have been happily chosen to designate a work coming from a mind so well fitted as his by constant communings with these divine compositions, fully to appreciate, and convey to others the heavenly aspirations of the "Sweet Singer of Israel." We find among his MSS. traces of this love in earliest boyhood, and in one of his prize Poems written in 1815, occurs the following fine paraphrase of the forty-sixth Psalm :—

> "God is our Hope and Strength! a present help
> In time of trouble! therefore though the earth
> Be moved, and her mountains 'midst the deep
> Be headlong tumbled, though the waters there
> Shall rage till every hill shall shake around
> We will not fear! The roaring winds and waves
> Shall only glad the dwelling of the Lord,
> The seat in which the Mightiest deigns to bide
> God in the midst forbids her to be moved!
> God shall assist her timely as before!
> The kingdoms threaten'd, and the proud of heart
> Combined in arms. But God gave forth His voice,
> Earth melted at the sound! The Lord of Hosts
> Is with us, Israel's Monarch is our shield!
> Come hither and behold His glorious works;
> What desolation in His wrath He brings

O'er all the earth ; what gladness when appeased !
See how He quells the storm of war, how breaks
The sword, and snaps the spear, exalts the weak,
And pulls the mighty down.   Be still then, Earth,
Tremble, ye kings, and know that I am God.
I will defend my people, I will bend
The stubborn knee of pride !   The Lord of Hosts
Is with us, Israel's Monarch is our shield !"

And even when all was changed, and the heavy
shadows of weariness and death hung around him,
his spirit still loved to linger amidst the songs of
Zion, and find in them expression for the humble
faith and quiet confidence, which smoothed his
dying pillow.

But while enumerating some of the features of
his parochial work, we must not omit to notice
his efforts to meet the peculiar requirements of
the fishermen and sailors who formed so large,
and, to him, so interesting a section of his
people. He visited them on board their vessels,
while in harbour as well as at their own homes,
and supplied every vessel with a copy of the Holy
Scriptures. For their use while at sea he composed
a brief manual of " Devotions," and, to assist in
giving a purer and healthier tone to their hours of
recreation, he wrote some naval songs, and adapted
them to popular times. Nor did he fail to give

them more direct religious instruction. He established a Sunday school on shore, to which he invited sailors of all ages; and here might be seen
together the old weather-beaten Man-of-war's man,
the hardy seaman in the prime of life, and the
reckless, laughing boy, all subduing for a time their
wilder natures, while listening to the stirring exhortations of their minister, or engaged in learning
to read the Holy Scriptures for themselves. But
it were scarcely possible, by the notice of a few
isolated facts, to give an adequate idea of the
happy relations which subsisted between the Pastor
and his flock. His frank, cordial tone in coming
amongst them ever gained a hearty response, and
the entire absence of all harshness, even in his
strong censure of sin, did not detract from their
affection and respect. The second Sermon in this
volume, preached at their own request, after a three
days' holiday on shore, by which, without drunk-
enness or disorder, they did honour to the accession
of our gracious Queen, was a proof at once of their
improved social tone, and the value justly set upon
their Minister's blessing. Nor was the effect of
this happy termination of their holiday merely temporary; it was the beginning of a custom, continued
among them through many after years, of coming
in a body to Church, when a special sermon was

preached to them, before leaving for their annual migration to fish off other parts of our coasts.

We will not, however, enter further into the details of our Author's parochial work, nor follow him through the varied scenes of his ministerial course, but will proceed at once to notice briefly the circumstances connected with the other three Sermons given in this volume, and the grounds for their selection. The first Sermon, headed "Without God in the world," was preached before Mr. Canning; and that great statesman was so much struck by its truth and force, as to request a private interview with the preacher, which was followed up by a brief but most interesting intercourse, from the tone of which, and the remembrance shown in later years, it were scarcely too much to hope that the good seed once sown was never afterwards wholly choked or trodden down. This sermon was selected, partly from the interest attaching to the great name with which it is coupled, and partly as having been written at an early date, and bearing internal evidence of a different tendency in the Author's mind from that which pervades the two last discourses—for, while the Editor would distinctly disclaim even the semblance of an attempt at controversy on a subject which has of late so agitated the public mind, it is not felt right to pass over in silence that gradual change, or rather development of religious views, which was clearly discernible in the latter years of our Author's life. We have previously noticed that at an early stage of his clerical life he embraced very deep and solemn views of religious truth, and the responsibilities of his sacred office. Earnestness and spiritual life did not then assume the form or take the line which they have since done, and these impressions were formed according to the received views of the so-called Evangelical clergy of the day. In their system the personal influence of the minister, rather than the legitimate authority of the Church, was the mainspring of action, and the various portions of the parochial system were carried out as the individual judgment of each Clergyman might deem best. The harmony of the Gospel, as set forth in the course of the Christian year by the Prayer Book, was not exhibited by the marked observance of the various sacred seasons as they came round, and but little was thought of those points in which our Church, as to position, privileges, authority, and definite system, stands on an entirely different footing from all sectarian bodies of Christians, and claims at once the affection and obedience of her children. This absence of definitive training, this want of a due recognition

of the duty of allegiance and affection to their
Church as to their spiritual mother in Christ, was
but little felt at a period when the great object of
religious teaching would seem to have consisted in
arousing the then dormant energies to any show of
vitality—but as the curse of a fallen nature is ever
shown in the corresponding abuse which mingles
with the use of all our best and brightest blessings,
so with the diffusion of spiritual life came also the
specious temptations of spiritual pride and error,
and thus arose a fresh need for some weapons and
safeguards against the threefold peril of "false
doctrine, heresy, and schism." This danger had
arisen, and this need was keenly felt by our Author,
while carrying on the work which we have already
briefly described; for though solid proofs were not
wanting that the blessing of God had rested on his
labours, yet when these temptations assailed his
people, they were, too often, found but ill prepared
to combat the plausible arguments, or resist the
flattering seductions with which they came in contact. They readily learned to turn aside from the
guidance of one whom they loved and honoured as
a man, but in whom they failed to recognize the
higher authority of a duly commissioned Ambassador
of Christ. They had not acquired such a spirit of
obedience as would induce them to submit their

own notions, and regulate their practices, by the decisions of primitive and apostolic rule. They had not been trained to love and confide in their Spiritual Mother—the Bride of Christ—and therefore, when other claimants to their regard arose, they were easily led captive, and not only forsook the home of their spiritual childhood, but as the false spirit of Antinomianism spread and strengthened, the faithful Minister saw many whom he had himself trained as lambs of Christ's flock, range themselves foremost in the ranks of schism, hostility, and even wild fanaticism*. And it was the gradual, though certain development of these painful results in the chief sphere of his labour, which led our Author eventually to modify his own views on the subject of religion: not that he ever really changed his opinions on the Articles of our Faith, or that he held less cordially the main truths of the Gospel, but he saw great reason to look differently on the mode of teaching them, and the general training of the members of Christ's flock, from

---

* This term was applied by our Author to the sect called " The Plymouth Brethren,"—who found especial favour among his people—in a letter, which we are unfortunately unable to give in full, but in which he gave to a pious friend who differed from him, a full statement of his later views, and the causes which had brought them forward.

what he had done in past years. Those who knew him best, will say that his love for Evangelical truth was as warm, as pure, as practical as ever; but he saw very clearly the need of combining with it that apostolical order which had been omitted in his earlier teaching. And it was not only the painful results which he witnessed in his own, and other parishes, that thus tended to modify his views of the truth, but other causes had prepared his mind for the gradual adoption of so-called Church principles, which having long been silently at work in his own mind, needed only some combination of circumstances to wake them into a living and active prominence amidst the elements of his teaching. During the hours spent in his extensive library, the formation of which had been for years his favourite recreation, he had made large acquaintance with the writings of the Fathers, and the earlier divines of the Anglican Church; having, by his wide Bibliographical research, enriched his stores with most of the best editions of the Fathers, and also accumulated a rare and valuable collection of the works of the Nonjurors, for whose quaint, severe, yet simple style, he possessed a peculiar relish, and had, at one time, partially prepared for publication, a new edition of their writings, with a history of their chief men and their times. In the

tone which much of the religious literature of the
day began at this period to assume, he recognized
many points already familiar to him; and from
personal acquaintance with some of the leading
modern writers on theological subjects, he was led
to turn his attention to the various publications of
the Oxford school, in whose writings he seems to
have found some of the defects pointed out in the
popular system of religious teaching, which had
forced themselves on his notice from the experience
of his own ministry. He found, too, drawn out
with distinctness, many of the leading truths and
features of the Church system, which had been
hitherto but slightly recognized by many of the
more earnest among the clergy, but which have,
within the last few years, exercised such wide and
deep influence throughout the whole body of the
Church. These principles—so far as they set forth
the fulness of Gospel truth, while the system of the
Church as the pillar and ground of the truth, was
exhibited in all the beauty of holiness and the simplicity of primitive faith—he made his own, believ-
ing, to use his own words, " That there was a
simple remedy provided, ready furnished to our
hands, in carrying out, fully and fairly, the principles and practices of our own Scriptural Church,
against either the fallacious refuge of Rome's

stagnant infallibility, or the irregularities and lati-
tudinarianism of those who would abrogate, as heart-
less formality, all attention whatsoever to Church
order and discipline;" and hoping also, that the dis-
semination of these principles might ultimately tend
to restore among his people those happy relations
between the various members of the body and their
Divine Head, which prevailed in apostolic times.
But it was not in the providence of God that His
servant should be spared to see the realization of
these hopes; for error had taken too deep root in
the rank soil to be easily or soon removed, and the
seeds of division and distraction, which had been
unconsciously sown in former days, grew up, and
brought forth their natural fruit.   In the first
bright days of promise and sanguine hope he had
looked for far other results at the close of his
ministerial labour; and though even in the calmer
hours of retrospect and thoughtful review he was
permitted, with the Apostle, to hope that he
had not " run in vain, neither laboured in vain,"
the choice of his text, when bidding his people
farewell before quitting England, and his mode
of dwelling upon it, speaks plainly of anxiety and
distress in the Pastor's heart, and of opposition,
division, and inconsistency, even then rife among
his people.   And these two discourses, the last he

ever composed, though they do not include a very
extended range of doctrine, may yet serve to point
out, in some measure, the growth and development
of our Author's views, and the change, if change it
can be called, in his system of religious teaching.
That it was not a change from practical to theo-
retical—from spirituality to formality—from liberality to uncharitableness—but, with an entire
simple dependance on the atoning sacrifice of our
Blessed Lord, earnest exhortations to growth in
grace, faith in God's promises, and practical prayer-
ful piety, through the help of the Holy Spirit,
there is coupled—a developed view of the responsibilities and privileges of those who have once been
admitted into the kingdom of Christ, a distinct and
definite recognition of the Sacraments as the appointed means of grace, and a strong plea for the
cultivation of such a spirit of union and concord
among themselves, as would prove them true
disciples of the Prince of Peace, having " one Lord,
one Faith, one Baptism, one God and Father of all."

We have already spoken of our Author's removal
from the scene of his labours ere he could watch
the progress of, or perfect, the efforts he made to
meet the difficulties which had arisen among his
people, and we may not speculate upon probabilities
which the good Providence of God has seen fit

to hide from our earthly vision; yet it were surely not well to turn aside from lessons, which the personal experience of this servant of God would teach us, or fail to treasure up such expressions of his ripened judgment as we gather from all later allusions to sacred subjects, and more especially from the tone of his last Hymn and Sermon, both written within very few weeks of his final release. During those trying months and years, when placed outside the circle of which he had ever been the life and centre, he bore no meaner witness to the reality and blessedness of his belief, by his cheerful resignation to God's will in suffering and weary sickness, than by the earnest consecration of his powers in past years to the more active duties of his sacred calling—and further, perhaps, another lesson may be gleaned from the records of his latter days,—when surrounded by the fascinations and allurements with which Rome so well knows how to attract an ardent and enthusiastic mind—and keenly alive to the many causes of perplexity and disquiet becoming daily more manifest in his own Communion, he yet never swerved from true allegiance to the Church of his Baptism, nor suffered his sympathy with some portions of the Romish system to mislead his judgment in its conscientious rejection of her vital errors— but found the faith which he professed and realized, sufficient, alike in life and death, to " lead him in

c 2

the paths of righteousness," and enable him to
enter fearlessly even the deep darkness of the
"valley of the shadow of death."

But we must turn from these suggestions, which
have led us too far in the course of our narrative,
and revert some years to the time when his strength,
overtasked, seemed gradually to be giving way. In
addition to the zealous discharge of his arduous
ministerial duties, the education of his children
engrossed much of his time, and for several years
he found it requisite to increase his income, and
avoid some of the evils of a strictly domestic education, by taking private pupils. He could not even
then relinquish the happiness he found in intellectual pursuits; he had ever, to use a phrase of his
own, "loved to hover about the confines of Par-
nassus," and it was only by straining his strength,
bodily and mental, to the utmost limit, by curtailed
rest, and incessant exercise of the mind, that he
was able to accomplish his numerous and varied
labours, and snatch a brief interval for such relaxation as would, of itself, have proved sufficient
employment for a less vigorous mind. Natural
science, in its various branches, possessed great
attractions for him, and in the peculiar features of
his loved and chosen home he had many facilities,
of which he gladly availed himself, for the in-
dulgence of these tastes. His mind was one which

could well dispense with those extraneous sources
of enjoyment which some find so needful to preserve
a healthy or cheerful tone—yet few more keenly
entered into the delights of cultivated society, or
were better qualified to take a prominent position
in the intellectual circle. He possessed a remarkable power of extracting something from every
mind, adapting himself without effort to those with
whom he came in contact, and infusing life and
animation where, without his help, they were least
discernible. His freshness and originality of thought,
his large amount of information, and his facility of
expression could not but attract attention, and
receive a welcome wherever they appeared;—yet he
was never led to overlook, or lightly value even
the smallest point of excellence in others by any
consciousness of his own superiority—rather, this
was most truly manifested in his own lowly estimate of powers, which all but he so highly prized.
He had small leisure, or opportunity however, for
the development of these qualities, or the cultivation of these tastes, whilst engaged in the all-
engrossing duties of his more active life. But his
day of labour was fast drawing to its close; eventide was coming on; and year by year, his bodily
frame seemed less equal to a pressure of occupations,
which no constitution, save one of extraordinary
physical and mental power, could have attempted.

In the spring of 1839, after some weeks of varied, yet almost nameless, suffering, he was induced to consult the celebrated Dr. Chambers, who at once told him that "unless he slackened his sails and cast anchor for a while, his voyage of life would soon be over." Yet there was no apparent disease, and even this warning awoke no serious alarm, and he shortly returned with renewed vigour, and unabated zeal, to his varied avocations.

Thus he continued to exhaust the remainder of his health and strength, with but brief intervals of relaxation [1], in the constant drudgery of teaching, and in parochial ministrations, or in satisfying the claims which were largely made upon his time and benevolence by the attention of friends and acquaintances, or the importunities of all who sought and found in him a ready friend and helper in their time of need. In the autumn and winter of 1843, being left for some months without assistance in his parochial labour, an attack of bronchitis followed his exposure to night air, and constant exertion of his lungs; and as his symptoms during the following spring daily assumed a more for-

---

[1] Some notes and letters, written during a brief summer tour in 1842, are given in the form of an Appendix; and such fragments are added of his correspondence from other parts of the continent, during the last three years of his life, as it is hoped will have interest for the reader.

midable character, he was at length compelled to follow the advice of his medical attendants, and to seek in a warmer climate, and at a distance from home, that bodily health and mental relaxation which he was unable to secure in England. For several months he had not attempted to undertake clerical duty, but before leaving home, late in the autumn of 1844, he preached the third sermon in this volume, and shortly after, amidst the mingled pain and comfort afforded him by the heartfelt expressions of regret from hundreds of his people, who watched his departure, he bade farewell to the happy home of many years. It was proposed that he should hasten to Naples, and there spend the winter months with his daughter—but the agitation of leave-taking, and the early bleak weather which set in while passing through France, were too much for his shattered constitution, and he was more than once compelled by illness to pause in his onward course. The lines headed " Longings for home," written after his arrival at Naples, touchingly tell us how fondly his thoughts still turned to England, and yet his natural buoyancy and elasticity of spirit would not allow either such regrets, or the unintermitted bodily suffering and confinement attendant on his illness, to destroy his flow of cheerfulness. During this winter he struggled with difficulty through more than one

severe attack, and his life was at one time in immi-
nent danger; but by the blessing of God on the
means used, and through the kindness and attention of those who ministered to his every want, he
was restored to some measure of strength, and was
enabled to leave the climate of Naples, which appeared unsuited to his health, and remove to Rome,
where he spent three months in comparative comfort,
though still in a very precarious state; no sooner,
however, did he recover, in any degree, from an attack,
than all his wonted energy returned, and he eagerly
sought to avail himself of the many sources of intellectual enjoyment opened in such rich profusion
in both ancient and modern Italy, until a violent
fever with which he was seized, after a week of un-
usual convalescence, and some consequent undue
exertion proved to him the danger which he incurred by any unwonted excitement. For a while
his life trembled in the balance,—and it may well be
conceived how grateful to his spirit, in this solemn
crisis, were the offices of his own Church, when
rendered to him with ready kindness, by a valued
clerical friend of former years. Some of his first
convalescent hours, were spent in composing the
poem, " Thoughts in Weakness," which sufficiently
expresses his then calm and peaceful frame of
mind. But his span of life was yet lengthened,
medical kindness and skill were permitted to

triumph over the fierceness of disease, and once more to build up the frail earthly tabernacle; and in the hope that lengthened rest and entire change might repair the inroads, which had been made on his constitution, the following summer was spent in wandering through the Tyrol and parts of Switzerland, where he was joined by his sons and other English friends; and when autumn came on he returned to Rome as his winter-quarters. The fluctuations of his health, his constant weakness and liability to sudden and sharp illnesses, rendered these journeys, but too often, very irksome and fatiguing. Yet his enthusiastic enjoyment of nature in all her aspects, his wonderful fortitude in suffering, and entire forgetfulness of self, and his natural playful exercise of wit and fancy, happily beguiled these hours of travel, and enabled him to reap fuller benefit than could have been anticipated from the change of air and scene. The trying season of winter passed over without any apparent progress of disease—on the contrary, his greater measure of health gave him a wider range of enjoyment, both in social and intellectual intercourse, and in exploring for himself some of the many objects of interest so thickly strewn around him.

Early in the spring of 1846, he left Rome for England, and spent a few months among his friends and family at Brixham. During his absence from

them, he had cherished the hope that he might
eventually be enabled to reside once more at his
own home, and though not to take any active part
in, yet, perhaps, to superintend, his former work in
the parish.   He found, however, that these hopes
rested on but a slight foundation; and he was
obliged to confine his exertions to a little private
intercourse with his parishioners, and to look forward to a further exile from the colder shores of
England.   His love of literature was as strong as
ever; and though subordinate to higher and holier
subjects of thought, occupied many of his leisure
hours.   He prepared, during the summer, an edition of the poems of Henry Vaughan, visiting the
beautiful vale of the Usk for the purpose of glean-
ing any local information of the Poet.   The fruits
of this summer tour are given in the biographical
sketch prefixed to his edition of Vaughan.   Had he
been spared, he hoped to have made this but the
commencement of a series of our early English
poets, with whose writings he was very familiar,
and whose beauties, he thought, would, even in this
unpoetical age, have attracted some attention.

The departure of summer, and the return of
symptoms which the least exposure to cold produced,
warned him to hasten southwards; and Italy was
again chosen, as being the country which at once
gave him the best hope of resisting his complaint,

and opened up to him the most numerous sources of interest, as an occupation for the mind. He somewhat varied this journey by a *détour* through some of the old towns of Lombardy, which he was anxious to visit, and arrived in Rome just as the cold weather commenced.

During a part of this, and most of the preceding winter, the investigation of such libraries as were accessible to him, was one of his greatest enjoyments; and the long evenings, necessarily spent in his own apartments, were also happily enlivened by the kindly visits of friends, and the study of those rare old folios, which he could not have seen elsewhere.

His muse, too, was not altogether idle; the events passing in Rome, in the winter of 1845, called forth the poem entitled, " The Czar in Rome," and the fragments of a fairy tale which follow this piece were written when his mind, sympathizing with the body then reduced to almost child-like weakness by severe illness, found a soothing relief in this simple, unstudied flow of rhyme.

It would be impossible to exaggerate the kindness which he met with at the hands of friends when alone in a foreign land; and surely even in impartial minds an interest must have been aroused for one whose protracted sufferings gave not to his character the faintest tinge of gloom or egotism, but were borne throughout with unvarying cheer-

fulness, patience, and resignation. It was said of
him, by one whose daily and intimate intercourse
cheered the last two winters of his life, "I have
often been struck by the exceeding resignation and
cheerfulness with which he bore all his sickness,
and the remarkable manner in which he was always
enabled to steer clear of every thing like egotism—
sickness has an almost inevitable tendency to make
persons egotistical and full of morbid self-con-
sciousness: this, however, was never his case. He
never volunteered to speak of himself as invalids
generally do; and when the subject was introduced
by others, and he was obliged to speak of self, he
did so with that graceful playfulness which evi-
denced in him a decided superiority of mind over
matter, and which caused every one who heard him
to feel tenfold that interest in the state of his
health which he did not seem to feel. I do not
know that I ever saw an invalid who had so successfully resisted, if indeed he was ever attacked
by, the peculiar temptations of delicate health.
Nothing but the power of the Holy Spirit, acting
on a peculiarly fine character by nature, could
have produced such a result; and this cheerfulness
and indifference about self did not result from in-
sensibility to, or ignorance of, his own state. He
was both fully alive to the hopeless character of
his illness and to the pain which every one must

feel who, after a useful and active life, (not merely many years of usefulness and activity,) is forced by Providence outside the social circle within which he had once been so energetic an actor. The change from being an actor to be a spectator is, to some minds, a greater trial than the change from health to sickness, of which it is a consequence."

Cut off from the active employments of former days, yet with all his powers of mind in full vigour, he much enjoyed such intellectual and social intercourse as his health permitted, with several of the clergy and laity of both the Anglican and Romish communions then resident at Rome, entering with almost painful anxiety into the occurrences of the times, and seeking, in his limited sphere, to temper, as far as might be, the rashness of some, and the controversial eagerness of others, by his own sobriety of judgment and forbearance of differences. And the source whence flowed these Christian graces was made plainly apparent in the utterance given in his later poems to the deeper musings of his quiet hours; indeed the tone of the pieces composed during the last few months of his life, and more especially of that on the New Year, and the hymn "Abide with me," give a blessed transcript of his inner mind, and would almost seem to breathe a prophetic prayer, which, ere a few short months or weeks had fled, was abundantly heard and answered.

In the spring of 1847 he was attacked with very severe illness, but he was unwilling to forego his return to England, and commenced his journey in so enfeebled a state, that it was thought necessary for his second son to meet him in the south of France, and accompany him home. He reached England much reduced in strength, and still more shaken in his whole system. Yet the wonderful elasticity of his spirits buoyed him up, and he was able each day, more or less, to enjoy the familiar, but beautiful, scenery around his chosen haunts, and once again, with affectionate delight, to take his place in the social circle, and by his cheerful tone and Christian spirit to diffuse the happiest influence over this brief period. On Midsummer-Day he officiated, in London, at the marriage of his second son, and gave the young couple his paternal, as well as ministerial, blessing with deep emotion; and after giving a short time to other friends at a distance, he returned to spend his last few weeks in England at Berry-Head, the spot of all others most dear to him from long and affectionate association. Here he lingered over the varied sources of heart felt interest which the home of many years supplied — his parish, his library, his garden—the very stones in and around the place where he had spent so many useful, happy days. Late in this summer he had a very serious attack of inflammation, which increased with such dangerous rapidity, that his life was despaired of: yet, even here, the merciful providence of God could be traced, in the unmistakeable evidence which this critical hour afforded to those who were not permitted to watch beside his dying couch, that God's Presence was indeed abiding with him—that He would "be his guide even unto death."

The summer was passing away, and the month of September (that month in which he was once more to quit his native land) arrived, and each day seemed to have especial value, as being one day nearer his departure, his family were surprised, and almost alarmed, at his announcing his intention of preaching once more to his people. His weakness, and the possible danger attending the effort, were urged to prevent it; but in vain. "It was better," as he used often playfully to say, when in comparative health, "to *wear* out than to *rust* out." He felt sure he should be enabled to fulfil his wish, and feared not for the result. His expectation was well founded. He did preach, and, amid the breathless attention of his hearers, gave them the Sermon on the Holy Communion, which is inserted last in this volume.—He afterwards assisted at the administration of the Holy Eucharist, and though necessarily much exhausted, by the exertion and excitement of this effort, yet his friends had no reason to believe it had been hurtful to him. In the evening of the same day he placed in the hands of a near and dear relative the little hymn, " Abide with me," with an air of his own composing adapted to the words.

Within a few hours after this, the little party, consisting of his second son, his wife, and a valued attendant, set out on their journey towards the genial south; a journey which he never completed, but which was ended by his peaceful entrance into that " rest which remaineth for the people of God."

Notwithstanding the illness we have already mentioned, he left England in some degree of health, and was able keenly to enjoy the society of his companions, and to point out each object of beauty or interest on their route. But within a few hours' journey of Nice, he was seized with influenza, which, soon after his arrival there, changed to dysentery, accompanied with very alarming symptoms.

He had so often, during the last few years, stood, as it were, on the very confines of eternity, that those around him hoped, even now, it might please God that this sickness should not be unto death; but in this hope he never participated, his ready perception foretelling but too truly the inevitably fatal result of such a disease upon a weakened frame, and putting aside from the first all expectation of recovery, he only earnestly entreated that no medicine might be given which would dim his faculties, nor any earthly concerns brought before him which could distract or debar him from holding constant communion with things unseen. For a few days bodily agony and mental depression sorely tried him, but the tempest and whirlwind ceased; the "still small voice" spoke peace, and as death came on at last slowly, but surely, it came visibly robbed of all its terrors. A peculiar blessing, and one which he prized full well, was vouchsafed to him in the counsels and ministrations of a brother clergyman of the Church of England, whose gentle, yet searching tone, peculiarly fitted him to be a chosen comforter in the hours of trial and pain. From his hands he received, for the last time, the Sacrament of the Lord's Supper, and it seemed as though, in the reception of that most precious Sacrament, all doubt, all disquiet, passed away,—he tasted of "that peace which passeth all understanding,"—his soul was stayed upon God, and neither the weakness of the flesh, nor the wiles of the evil one, had any power to rob him of that strong confidence. Yet there was nothing vain-glorious, nothing scenic in his death-bed. "From pride, vain-glory, and hypocrisy" he fervently prayed to be delivered; and while his few words all breathed of peace and hope, they were mingled with the deepest humility. "He had nothing,—was nothing, in himself." "He gloried

d

not save in the cross of our Lord Jesus Christ,"—
" a sinner saved by grace,"—" a brand plucked from
the burning," yet clothed in spotless raiment, washed
in a Saviour's blood, and owning an unfading in-
heritance, " eternal in the heavens." The character
of his complaint rendered it necessary often to administer powerful opiates during the first few days of
his illness, and their lowering and stupefying influence often distressed him; being jealous of every
moment not given to the God he was so soon to meet,
and fearful lest his mind might not remain unclouded
to the last; but in this, as in other instances, his
prayers were heard, and his desires fulfilled; his
mind never wandered, and long after no sound
passed his lips, he gave clear signs that none of his
faculties were dulled or dead. Through life he had
always shrunk with nervous apprehension from the
act of dying, but now this terror did not harass
him, though he used frequently to beseech his God,
if it might be his will, to grant him a quiet release
from the fetters of clay which detained him here.
His whole soul seemed so imbued with peace and
hope, that the last agony and the darkness of the
grave dwelt not in his thoughts. One day, on
waking from sleep, he said to his faithful attendant,
"Oh! there is nothing terrible in death; Jesus Christ
steps down into the grave before me." And in his
case there was nothing terrible; no agony at the

last. His prayer was heard, and when his summons came, without a sigh or a struggle, he literally fell asleep in Jesus.

Within three days of his first seizure his medical attendants had given up all hopes of his recovery, and announced that death was very near; yet for days he lingered, and his hour of release came not; but, through the long days and weary nights of an almost living death, his patience, fortitude, and cheerfulness, never forsook him; no word of complaint or impatience ever passed his lips, but as he lay there, dying in a distant land, life slowly ebbing away, the pallor of wasting sickness cast over all things, he would tenderly and gratefully mark each comfort which affection and solicitude provided; and, still noting, as had ever been his wont, the varied beauties of morn and even, spread over a southern sea and sky, he would thankfully record the mercies which his God had showered round his path in each stage of life, and now no less in death; and as " earth's vain shadows " fled, and the light of " heaven's morning " broke upon his soul, even these faint traces of earth, so bearing the hue of heaven, passed away, and his spirit mounted as on eagle wings upwards to those mansions prepared for such as have " fought a good fight," who " have finished their course, who have kept the faith," "and for whom henceforth there is laid up a crown of glory which fadeth not away." His soul seemed filled with a sense of the nearness of his God, too high and blessed for mortal participation. His lips constantly moved as if in joyful converse, while no sound was heard; and as those near him would strive to discern his import, he would motion them away, murmuring, " peace, joy," and pointing upwards with his own bright, beaming smile, to where he held communion with things unseen. Oh! blessed converse! begun on earth, to be perfected so soon in Paradise! Blessed faith! to-day piercing through the mists of earth! to-morrow changed to sight! "abiding ever with the Lord." On Saturday, the 20th of November, he "entered into rest." "Blessed are the dead that die in the Lord; yea, saith the Spirit, for they rest from their labours."

A simple marble cross in the English cemetery at Nice fitly marks the last earthly resting-place of one whose highest honour and desire in active life had been to exalt the Cross; who meekly bore the Cross through years of suffering, and who, trusting in the merits of his Blessed Saviour's Cross and Passion alone, calmly resigned his mortal life, in the sure and certain hope of a glorious immortality.

A. M. M. H.

Berry-Head, 1850.

APPENDIX.

APPENDIX.

It may appear strange that in the preceding Prefatory Memoir no quotations have been made from any journals or private memoranda. A very simple circumstance will however explain this omission. Among our author's MSS. was found a note strongly expressive of his desire that no journals which he had left undestroyed should ever be made public; regarding any idea of possible publicity attached to such records as depriving them of their strictly private and sacred character. This prohibition does not, we conceive, extend to his letters; and though from his usually stationary life whilst in health, and the effort which correspondence became to him in illness, we have but few of these to offer, it has been thought that such extracts as can be given would be of interest to his friends. It need scarcely be premised that neither these extracts, nor any others contained in the Memoir, were written with any idea of being published, and are only given as more faithfully representing the man himself in the familiar undress of affectionate family intercourse, than many words from any other pen than his own could do. Yet it is obvious that the very small portion necessarily given of the whole unreserved correspondence can but faintly pourtray his true relish for beauty, in all its forms—whether exhibited in art or nature; his romantic love of adventure, his lively sallies of playful wit, or (far beyond these) the deep tide of home affections, which alike characterized his conversation and correspondence.

The first part of the Appendix consists of letters and notes written in and from Norway, when in the enjoyment of health and strength, and, though incomplete in themselves, are given as happily illustrative of his usual graphic and lively style of descriptive writing.

The second part is composed rather of fragments than of letters, written from Italy, and turning chiefly on topics of the day, but also exhibiting the cheerful patience with which he bore his sufferings, and giving us at times glimpses of his inner life, though this he ever shrank from laying open even to the eyes of friends.

PART I.

Letters and Notes descriptive of a Tour in Norway during the Summer of 1842.

"Norway, off Christiansand, Aug. 15, 1842.

" KNOWING how manifold are the engagements that usually await one at the close of one's journey, I begin to pen a line to you, while yet on board of the steamer that is bearing us fast to ' Norway's foamy strand.' The whole line of that stupendous coast, 900 miles of bleak and stormy cliffs, is frowning at this moment on us, after one of the most delightful of voyages to reach it. We left Hull at twelve on Saturday morning, firing off our two signal guns amid hundreds of gazers on the pier, and since then, we have had little more wind than would raise a ripple on the surface of the deep. On Sunday I gave the whole ship's company Divine service on the deck, and even the uneasiest sailor on the ship acknowledges, from the experience of this voyage, that it is possible to prosper, even with a parson on board—the general impression, you know, among them is, that ever since Jonah sailed from Tarshish, the presence of a man of God is unpropitious on board of ship : but now, strange

to say, they have never had so speedy and prosperous a voyage as the present."

" Monday Evening, Aug. 15.

" To-day at four p. m., when I began this letter,
we reached Christiansand, in Norway, and landed to
deliver the mail and a few bales of goods there, and
are now breasting the blue waters again on our
way to Gottenburg, where we hope to arrive in
about nine hours. Christiansand is a beautiful little
clean town, situated at the bottom of one of the
noble fiords of this country, backed on every side
by fine rocky hills, sprinkled over with firs. The
whole region around is ' glorious in desolation.'
Mountains of granite 9000 feet high rushing up
into the clouds, and extensive island masses of rock
lining the whole coast. The people appear a fine
vigorous race, that inhale a freeborn air, and feel
the sea to be their native element. I could easily,
as I saw their little boats dashing across the Bay
we entered, imagine how their forefathers pushed
their pinnaces through the foam to invade and subdue the shores of England and other parts of Europe.
When on shore at Christiansand we went to the
house of the principal merchant of the place, who
has a garden in which are grown many of the
flowers of England, as well as some of our fruits.

They have currants, gooseberries, strawberries, and apples, and among the flowers I recognized the Chrysocoma of Berry-Head. We then rambled to the Cathedral, for the place is a Bishopric, and entered a remarkable old building, with very little of Gothic about it, but a kind of Tartar style reigning within. There was an altar curiously ornamented with marble figures in alto relievo, and candles on the table. The minister also wears a stole of rich crimson velvet and a large cross on the back of his surplice. What will K. say to this in Protestant Sweden? We are just arrived at Gottenburg, and are working into the picturesque harbour."

" Köngsberg, Norway,
Finished Aug. 29, 1842.

* " I begin another letter to you, though as yet I have received none from you, or any one else in England. . . . . I have persuaded H. to set out with me, on a little tour through Sweden and Norway. We went therefore into Gottenburg, purchased a carriage, or rather dog-cart, and set out the second day after I arrived. Our first stage

---

* The Editor does not undertake to answer for the correct orthography of the local names, which it is almost impossible to decipher in the original MS.

was up the river Gœtha (which is pronounced Euta)
by steamboat to the splendid falls of *Trolhalten*.
We passed through beautiful scenery, composed, as
the greater part of that in Sweden is, of granite
hills of a beautiful purple colour, covered with wood,
and between them rich verdant plains, forests, and
lakes. The scenery is fine and striking beyond
any thing that I know of. *Trolhalten*, however,
itself left all that I ever saw far behind. A greater
body of water than the Rhine rushes down over
rocks twice as high as Schaffhausen, foaming, dashing, roaring all the way, and you can approach the
fall so near as almost to ' lay your hand upon his
mane.' From hence we took carriage to *Udevalla*,
three Swedish miles distant, but a Swedish mile,
you must know, is seven English, and a Norwegian
nearly eight. As H. speaks Swedish well we had
no difficulty in getting on, but he, poor fellow, is
not strong and well; and we could seldom get on
our road till eleven or twelve o'clock—and then,
what with a blazing sun, and dust, and hill after hill,
and roads knee-deep in sand, with an agreeable ad-
mixture of rocks, and large stones and roots of trees
stretching across the way, we made but little progress. We contrived, however, on the fourth day to
reach Norway, and crossed there an arm of the sea to
Holmestrand. We were six hours in getting over,

and it blew hard, so that our carriage was in a little
jeopardy once or twice. We reached *Holmestrand*
however soon after midnight. . . . .
Our intention on setting out was to go from hence
straight into the middle of a fine mountainous
region near, called the *Gousta;* but H., distrusting
his powers of speaking Norse, which he can do very
tolerably, wished to change our route, and we went
to the town of *Drammen*, a very fine, but dear,
place, where we were well fleeced by the smooth-
spoken landlord, who talks English, and makes his
guests pay for it. We called there on a Mr. H.,
a Scotchman, settled in the place, and he kindly
gave us a route in a new direction, to *Hongsund*,
Vigersund, *Beersund*, the *Sperillan Soe*, or lake,
and on to *Nas*, at the head of it. This took us
into the middle of a fine region, called *Ringe Rigi;*
and the lake, I think, surrounded by magnificent
conical hills, exceeds any thing I saw in Switzerland,
and made me long to penetrate farther into the
country; H., however, was so poorly, that we were
here obliged to turn back, and we went on by slow
journeys to *Honenfoss*, where the landlord speaks
English. . . . . . . Here one of H.'s dogs
strayed away, and we spent a day in looking
after her in vain; but as she was a valuable setter,
H. determined to stay there for a few days, in

order to find her ; and I thought it better to move
about a little, and see the country in the mean-
time, appointing a rendezvous with him at Christiansand.   H. declares I shall be lost, travelling by
myself, without being able to speak a word of
the language, and my experience hitherto has not
been encouraging.   I was out last night on a lake
till four in the morning, before I reached a place to
sleep ; and to-day I have only got on seven English
miles as yet, and it is past four in the afternoon.   But
I hope to improve as I go on ; and I have a direction in my pocket if any thing should happen, where
the people are to send me ; and I find them good-
natured, if we could only understand one another.
If I come quite to a stand still, I have one resource
—to get to the nearest Lutheran priest (all of
whom speak Latin), and get his assistance.   I shall
hope to give you, in my next, a little more of
Norway, especially the wilder parts of it, that is, if
I get on at all, as I hope to do ; and also some
little sketches of the manners and customs of the
people."

                                    " Aug. 28th.

" I write from *Hongsund,* whither I came in a
carriole without springs.   This was, however, reme-
died by my air-cushion, which has been a grea
object of curiosity along the road.   The landlord

here determined to make money of me. He could not get post-horses for me under two hours, but had one of his own, which I might have immediately, at three times the proper charge. Well, I hired it, and thought, now at least I shall get on. But mine host first went and got his dinner; then took off the wheels of the carriole and greased them; then sent for the horse to a field; then curried him; then fed him; and, at the end of two hours, took me for three times the proper price. I was indignant, and looked as angry as I could, but I could not speak a word. I then pushed on to *Köngsberg*, a very nice little place, and came to the best inn I have seen in Norway. The servants are nice quiet girls, and every thing seems to be conducted with propriety and regularity. I got supper, and a good bed; coffee, as usual, at seven in the morning: but Captain G., my great stay at this place, is not at home, and I cannot get a vocabulary, or make the people understand any thing but ' Let me have breakfast, a bed, and a horse.' Still I mean to press on to the *Gousta* Mountains, and across the country to Christiansand. The landlord here, *Christiansen*, is a fine fellow; I wish he could speak a little English, but he cannot, so we are obliged to converse by signs."

" Monday.—*Köngsberg*. Had much difficulty in getting on, but sent to secure one Christian Hintell as a guide. He would not come without being paid for it—or rather, as I found afterwards, he feared that his English would break down. However, I went to him, and contrived to exchange a few words, and arranged to take him to *Gousta*. I then went to Mrs. G., a very sweet woman; and from her to Dr. B., with Director S., who took me to the Mint, to Mr. L., a most intelligent man, a mineralogist and antiquarian; his eye all fire, and his countenance all intelligence. They drew up for me a route to *Gousta*, while I went with Hintell to the silver mines. They are about five miles from *Köngsberg*, high in the side of a hill. We entered by a long tunnel, about a mile in length, with a strong breeze blowing through it, which made it difficult for the men to carry their torches. The water, in many places, roared under us. We descended the ladders to the working place, 800 feet, and saw the silver *in situ*. The lode runs from east to west, and is about seven or eight feet wide. The men work with hand-borers and hammers, and then blast. Their wages are about a mark a day, and they work twelve hours. The ore appears very rich; one piece which was shown to me was, as the director informed us, more than 50 per cent. The toil of ascending was terrific. I drank nearly a gallon of water from the springs by the way, and felt the cold air much in the tunnel. However, I got back to my comfortable inn in good time, and after my *quelmot* and a bottle of ale, went to bed much fatigued.

"Tuesday.—Off at six, after coffee, to *Gousta*. We plodded slowly to H———, where we had lunch at a farmer's house; one of the most curious in antiquities that I have seen. The English royal arms were enamelled in the middle of one of the brazen dishes, and all the furniture was of the most antique description. There was an old Danish Bible of 1532 in folio, with a beautiful title with Frederick II. on the reverse, and in splendid condition; I longed to buy it, but there was no possibility of carrying it off. The farmer, with his father's father, had inhabited for generations this singular building, which, with all its out-houses, was carved and painted in the most grotesque manner, without and within. From hence, we went on roughing it indeed over the most execrable roads to *Bamble*. We stopped on the way to visit a most singular old wooden church at *Kitterdal;* I never saw so extraordinary a building. The oldest parts have all the appearance of having belonged to an Idol

e

Temple, there being no emblems of Christianity in
any part of the carving, the rest however is pro-
fusely ornamented with crosses, both without and
within. The Clergyman is a fine open counte-
nanced affable man, who speaks a little English, and
a little more Latin. At *Bamble*, having sent
Hintell back to look for my fly book, which a boy
stole while I was viewing the Church, I was almost
starved before I could get the old lady to bring me
a little cooked water for tea; there were eggs, and
other eatables I believe in the house, but, alas, I
could not order them, so I took my tea, and a piece
of bread, and went to bed.

" Wednesday.—A wet morning. It cleared up,
however, at ten o'clock, but it was only a temporary
truce. We set out, and there came on a terrific
thunder-storm : the roaring of the thunder through
the hills—*Gousta's* last shout; the rain, not in
drops, but in bucketfulls; the rivulets all tor-
rents;—verily, a noble scene among the mountains
and forests : but wet to the skin; and the jolting
of the cart terrible, with the horses wanting to
fight. At length we reached *Tindoset*—a poor
place; but they lighted a fire, at which we dried
our clothes; and then I wrote a Latin letter to the
priest for flies, and received, in addition to a noble
supply of my wants, a most courteous reply."

"August 35, 1842.

" I sit down to fulfil the promise I gave you in my last letter, of letting you have a sketch of the manners and customs of the people among whom I have been living for the last week or two. . . I am, on the whole, favourably impressed with the people of this country. The peasants appear to be a sturdy, straightforward, vigorous race, most of them nearly six feet high, with good open countenances, and very respectful to their superiors. I never pass one that he does not take off his hat, and he universally holds it in his hand, while speaking to you.

" The higher orders also appear to be a polite, yet independent and manly race, and the middle class, farmers, shopkeepers, and innkeepers, are, as in most places, very diversified. One is not likely indeed to meet the best specimens of a nation on their roads, and at their hotels, and the persons who keep the inns here are generally broken-down merchants or other such persons, and do not stand high among their countrymen ; and of those whom I have met with, their mercenary ways beat all I have experienced elsewhere. The women are generally plain—the peasants nearly as black and sunburnt as Italians, owing, I suppose, to their exposure to such a scorching sun in summer, and nine months of smoke in winter. They all, however, have beautiful hair, and appear to take great pains with it. It is always light in colour, and that of the children universally white. The girls of every grade wear it, either in long plaits, or flowing about their shoulders, and it becomes them exceedingly. There is no peculiarity in dress, of parts of Sweden which I have visited, save that the women of the lower order universally go about with a handkerchief tied round their heads instead of bonnets, and the men have all a large silver brooch for their shirts, and their frieze coats are curiously bordered with velveteen, and have a kind of epaulette of the same material on the shoulder. All the people of the middle and lower classes go about at this season without shoes or stockings, and the young women have little more on them than a petticoat. The mode of living here is rather curious. Among the bettermost people, the day begins with a cup of coffee, with rusks, which you find every where excellent, as well as the coffee, and a glass of brandy after them. This they bring you before you get out of bed, generally about six or seven in the morning. Then you dress, and about nine comes *furcast* or breakfast, consisting of meat, eggs, fish, ale, &c., with the eternal accompaniment of brandy. About one or two o'clock you get *mittag* or dinner,

consisting of hot joints, fowls, &c., and abundance
of strong drinkables. And, lastly, you have *quelmot*
or supper, about six, another very substantial meal,
with tea and brandy again, if you like, after it.
The worst feature of the eatables to me, is that
they all come up raw: you have raw fish, raw
bacon, raw sausages, and raw smoked beef; and
they stare at you, if you ask them to broil any of
them. The poor people appear to live very hard,
on bread made partly of rye and partly of oats,
and sometimes of birch bark. However, they have
generally *flat-brode*, cakes of oatmeal and rye, thin
as a wafer, like Scotch bannocks, and very good
milk and potatoes. By the bye, they always give
you scalded cream with your coffee, or rather they
boil up the milk, cream and all, for the purpose.
The inns are generally very bad, and the beds in
this hot weather insufferable. They have no bed-
clothes, save a sheet and a feather-bed over it,
which may be comfortable enough in winter, but
it is intolerable in summer; the beds too are generally populous, and the gnats or mosquitoes trouble-
some at night. The Pastoral office appears to be
pretty well filled here, and the people on the whole,
especially in the country places, duly respectful to
their minister. Schools exist every where, and the
Pastors once a month have the children all brought

before them, and examine them as to their pro-
ficiency. I have been at church twice since I
came here; and once, on a week-day, saw the
Sacrament of the Lord's Supper administered.
The Clergymen on all these occasions, had splendid
voices, and went through the service extempo-
raneously, the people reading after them from
their prayer books, which appear not unlike our
own. The service seemed to be much diversified,
no part lasting more than a few minutes without a change of posture, and, I suppose, of
matter. The sermon, if it might be so called,
appeared to be delivered at intervals, between the
other parts of the service; and baptisms were performed during the same time. However, understanding little or nothing of what was said, I could
only look on and guess."

PART II.

Fragments of Letters from Italy, and other parts of the Continent, between the years 1844 and 1847.

"Leghorn, Nov. 12, 1844.

" MANY thanks for all the news you have sent me —all news from England are acceptable, but most of all news from home and its neighbourhood. There my thoughts all still harbour, and there still find their pivot and centre. Indeed I have not hitherto had very much to draw them elsewhere. I have been too ill to visit or take any interest in the various attractive objects around me. My week at Avignon, which was to have been given to Roman remains and papal palaces, was spent in bed. At Lyons the case was no better. I enjoyed the blue mountains, closed by Mont Blanc, that ennobled our voyage down the Rhone, and I gasped and tottered through a palace or two at Genoa; but all the rest has hitherto been sickness and suffering, weakness and exhaustion. This is but a sorry report, and ought not to be sent to you, save as an apology for past silence. . . . I am not worse to-day, though I fear not much better, and am obliged to look at others moving off by the steamers, without the power of accompanying them. I sometimes think that I am near the end of my journey altogether; but I hang on the goodness and mercy of God, and amid the watches of the night enjoy some comfortable meditations on His pardoning love, His restoring grace, His protecting providence. Yes, blessed be God, I can commit myself, soul and body, to His hands."

"Naples, Jan. 19, 1845.

"How it will be with me eventually, I scarcely dare to anticipate; but I much fear that I shall not see Berry-Head again. However, I can meekly bow, and say, 'The Lord's will be done,' and can trust in a Saviour's merits to give one of His unworthiest of creature's acceptance with God. This indeed is all my hope, and all my desire; and well, perhaps, is it for me, that I have no merits of my own to detain me from reposing thus exclusively on the blood of a Redeemer: I have been kept also, I trust, in a patient spirit throughout my illness, and receive it as an earnest of God's love, that He has withheld me, through all my sufferings of so many months, from uttering one word of impatience or repining. Perhaps I ought here to close; but I cannot do so without abundant thanks to you for your last dear, valued little letter. It was indeed a *multum in parvo*—every one of its details full of interest: and it did me more good, I believe, than all the medicine I took that day."

"Naples, Jan. 31, 1845.

"In leaving Naples, of which I have seen but little, owing to my tedious illnesses, I cannot help again and again longing that *you* could see a little of it as well as myself. In spite of its filth, it would still divert you: every thing seems so full of life. Even the old Romish church must, I should think, be very different from what it is elsewhere. It is certainly any thing but dead here. We have nothing but earnest extempore preaching on every side of us. Every Sunday afternoon a priest stations himself in the street under one of our windows, and preaches for a good hour to the assembled multitude. The emotions exhibited by the bystanders on these occasions are most extraordinary; tears often flowing down every face, and the most intense interest manifested on every side. The whole neighbourhood also appears to swarm with Sunday-schools, and adults as well as children attend them; and when they are over, the whole march together, singing hymns, through the streets, from the school, I believe, to the church, where, I imagine, they are dismissed to their homes. All this is very unlike any thing I ever expected to meet with in the Church of Rome, and indeed very inconsistent with other things that I could mention. Preaching, however, I find, and always extempore, universal in the churches, especially those of the Jesuits."

"Naples, Feb. 5, 1845.

" In a few days, however, we shall start for Rome. How the air of the Eternal City will agree with me remains to be proved. They tell me that the sea is injurious to me. I hope not; for I know of no divorce I should more deprecate than from the lordly Ocean. From childhood it has been my friend and playmate, and never have I been weary of gazing on its glorious face. Besides, if I cannot live by the sea, adieu to poor Berry-Head—adieu to the common, the rocks, and military ruins—adieu to the wild birds and wild flowers, and all the objects that have made my old residence so attractive. However, I must not go on, or I shall fall into my old croaking style again."

"Rome, Feb. 16, 1845.

"In spite of my suffering, I greatly enjoyed the journey hither. For the greater part of the way, the road wound among the Appennines: immense blocks of rock filled the valleys and hill-sides, along which we passed; and these again were clothed with olives and vines, and orange and lemon trees, beautifully blending the wild and the cultivated. Here a noble peak presented itself covered with snow, and there a ruined aqueduct stalked across a valley. In one place we broke upon the glorious sea, dashing against the walls of some picturesque old tower, and in another caught sight of one of these fantastic and castellated piles, standing on the spur of one of the surrounding mountains, or commanding some rugged pass between them; and Fondi, Mola di Gaeta, and Terracina, towns on the road, are each worthy of a painter. With regard to Rome, it will, I fear, be some time before I can tell you much of it: great kindness, however, we have already experienced here, as well as every where else. ———— is profuse in his offers of kindness. Truly, as P. says, if we ever exercised hospitality or showed kindness to any one at Berry-Head, it has been more than repaid to us here, in our day of need, in Italy."

"Rome, March, 1845.

"This place is certainly as different from Naples as one place can be from another. There the chief interest is to be found in the beautiful scenery, and the supple and versatile people; here the people are comparatively grave and dignified, and the great interest of the place arises from its associations. You spoke of the excitement attending the first view of the Eternal City, and it was very great. I had not expected to see it in all its ruined splendour, seated as it is in a mighty plain. I had imagined it somehow lying in a mountainous district; but, like London, Paris, and, I believe, all other great cities, it lies in a vast basin, with mountains rising all around; but generally at the distance of from ten to fifteen miles from the city."

"Rome, April 16, 1845.

" Praised be God that the hand which pens this is not cold in the grave! I have had another deliverance from death; a more wonderful one than any that has preceded it. For some time past I have been daily failing; but on Sunday week one of these terrible Italian fevers, that knock a man down like a bullock, pounced on me, and in a few hours my life was not worth a day's purchase. ·. . .

" On Saturday, when I felt dying, it was a great comfort to me to have Mr. B. to read and pray with me, and administer the Lord's Supper—the pledge and earnest of His pardoning love. Oh! what it

was to me then to be able to look to Him, and to
trust all to His power and goodness. . . . . .

"All this time, while there was an under-current
of the deepest earnestness and seriousness, there
was a constant play above it of the most fantastic
drollery. This was the turn imagination seemed to
take. All kinds of quips, and cranks, and conun-
drums went dancing through my brain; and many
of them found utterance from my tongue. . . .
I made more verses, I believe, and some of them, I
fancy, not bad ones, than would have filled volumes,
though now not a wreck, not a scrap, or scarce a
scrap, remains."

"Rome, May 1, 1845.

"I hope to pen you a few lines, better worth
sending, when I am stronger — if indeed that is
ever to be; and if not, thanks be to the Saviour of
Sinners, I am, I hope, better prepared to meet His
gracious will than I was. My late illness has, I
trust, been not without its blessing, and taught me
to realize things that we are too much accustomed
to hold as theories. However, I would speak
tremblingly on these topics. I know my weakness, and the strength of besetting sins; and ought,
I feel, to be humble and cautious. Pray for me,
my dear friend. Indeed I know you do so, and it
is no small comfort to be assured of the fact."

"Venice, June 11, 1845.

" Nothing can give the slightest idea of this Queen of the Waters; and on the evening of the regatta, when every house and palace along the grand canal was hung with tapestry, and thousands of beautiful gondolas, many with ten rowers, and all dressed out in the most brilliant and fanciful costumes, were gliding along the waters swift as darts, and yet not one interfering with the other, the scene was one which beggars all description: I never witnessed any thing the least like it—so brilliant and so novel. Indeed Venice itself is the most lovely spot I was ever in; and the evening trips that we take in our gondolas out into the offing to catch the evening sea-breeze are more luxurious than you can imagine."

"Rome, March 7, 1846.

" Even a little talking I often find too much for me, and I therefore go about like a monk of La Trappe, dropping into book-shops and libraries, when I find any warm enough for me, and conversing much, both there and at home, with the mighty dead through their writings. You would be surprised to hear what folios I have perused since I came to Italy; but I have much time for study, as I have not, since I left England, been once, willingly, out of my house after sun-set. It is a great privation to me, that I cannot write. The labour of composition I find makes me ill, and the act of stooping over paper, for the purpose of writing, likewise pains and injures me. However, I have abundant reason for thankfulness that I am as I am. No person that knew me last year could have anticipated my surviving to this spring, and yet here I am with another and other respite granted to me."

"Basle, Aug. 30, 1846.

"Much of our route through Belgium was different, or made in a different way, from that which we took in days of yore. The railroads have annihilated the long and dreary drive from Brussels to Cologne. . . . We saw the top of the tower, under which Charlemagne was found sitting in sepulchral state at Aix, but did not intrude on his ghostly solitude. Even old Cologne, with its half-finished, or, rather, half-commenced cathedral, is scarcely what it was, now that its echoes are startled by the railroad whistle. Still, though steam has done much to change the aspect of things in these quarters, enough remained unchanged to bring back very lively reminiscences of days gone by; and P. was edified, as we passed

along, with sundry anecdotes and observations on
those our maiden days of travel and foreign adventure together. We arrived at Antwerp on Friday,
after a still, but roasting, passage, and took up our
quarters at *our* old Hotel de St. Antoine. They
are beautifully repairing the cathedral tower, and
fitting up the interior of the choir with carved oak,
in the best taste. I mean, they are doing it in real
Gothic style, and not filling it with huge wooden
histories, such as the Creation, Adam, Eve, and all
the birds and beasts, nearly as large as life; or the
Conversion of St. Paul, with the heavens opening
above, and the rocks rending below, and St. Paul
and his horse sprawling between them. Such un-
wieldy sculptures, however difficult to execute,
have no charms for me, and no suitability, I think,
to a fine Gothic edifice, and yet the Belgic churches
are full of them, both in wood and stone. They
are, however, beginning to go back in their carv-
ings to an earlier and better school, and those
that are now going on at Antwerp are quaint and
minute, and in perfect keeping with the older and
better parts of the building."

"Vicenza, Sept. 16, 1846.

"I have been pursuing my intention of zigzagging
about among the fine old cities in Lombardy, and

they have in no respect disappointed my expecta-
tions. Brescia, and Verona, which I left yesterday,
and this Vicenza likewise, are most interesting
places, full of beautiful and curious architecture of
all ages, and rich in fine churches and paintings.
This is in fact quite a city of palaces, and the
wonders of Palladio's hand, and the influence of
his style, are to be seen on every side. No one,
indeed, knows any thing of Italy till he has rum-
maged out these repositories of her past glories."

"Milan, Oct. 12, 1846.

"For the next month we shall, I hope, be on the
move, exploring the cities on the south of the
Po; Piacenza, Parma, Reggio, Modena, Bologna,
Ravenna, &c.

"I have been so highly interested with my
Lombardie trip, that I am full of hopes as to
the other. The old towns of Lombardy, turned
out to be by far the cleanest, brightest, and
most interesting places I have seen in Italy. We
have hardly had a creeping, or buzzing, or
skipping thing throughout our journey, save the
mosquitoes at Padua and Venice. Brescia is a
most charming place, full of its own distinguished
painters, built half of its extent on Roman
foundations, with a bronze statue of 'Victory,'

f

rivalling any at Rome, and a picture by Paolo
Veronese, the Death of St. Aphia, alone worth
travelling twenty miles to see. Then Verona, rich
in Roman and mediæval remains, with half a dozen
noble churches, left just as they came from the
hands of their builders in the eleventh century, full
of splendid equestrian monuments of the Scaligeri,
and surrounded with battlemented walls climbing
over the neighbouring heights. The magnificent
amphitheatre supplies just what is wanting in the
Coliseum at Rome. The interior is almost perfect, and
there are three fine Roman gates, pretty much what
they were when Ausonius trotted through them.

"Mantua is a less interesting place, except to
those who study fortification. However, one must
go thither to learn what Giulio Romano can do, as
a painter, and, indeed, as an architect likewise.
There is a Morning, Noon, and Night, by him, on
the ceiling of the great room in the Corte Impe-
riale, that is very noble, especially 'the Night,' with
her dusky chariot and steeds. 'The Noon' consists
of a Jupiter amongst the gods on Olympus. Murray
does not seem to have understood that this was
the classical mode of representing mid-day. The
palace of Te, however, a little outside of Mantua,
is Giulio's *chef d'œuvre*, and certainly never did a
rich, exuberant, voluptuous imagination run riot as

his does there. Cremona again overflows with fine pictures, though they are fast modernizing away all the interest of the old churches. Murray, I think, never could have visited the place, for he leaves the finest of its churches, full of splendid pictures, St. Pietro, wholly unmentioned. There is a picture there which was carried to Paris, and restored at the peace; and a Madonna, with a figure kneeling beside her, by an old master, Bonifacio Bembo, at the church of St. Angelo, is one of the loveliest pictures I ever looked on. Lodi has only one church worth visiting, the Incoronata; but this is a gem indeed; full of the loveliest pictures, either by Titian or in Titian's best style. The town is worth a visit from Milan for these alone."

"Rome, Nov. 25, 1846.

" At last, I write to you again from Rome. After long wanderings, much of toil and sickness, here I am once more, through Divine mercy, in a quiet resting-place, for some months to come. Before my arrival here, some kind friends had taken for me a comfortable residence on the Pincian Hill, the last house of the Via Gregoriana, only one story high, so that I have no trouble in getting up stairs, and overlooking all the beauties and glories of modern Rome. How I wish that I could place you

f 2

here for a few minutes at my side, and, as your eye
wandered over the cupolas, and spires, and pillars,
and domes below, give you the history of each, with
all the interesting associations, classical, ecclesiastical, and romantic, that are attached to them ! . . .

"I find Rome much altered, I mean, as to the
prevailing tone of feeling. The old 'semper
eadem' system is gone altogether, under the
auspices of the new Pontiff, and improvement is
the order of the day in all things *but one*. They
diligently adhere to usage in ecclesiastical matters ;
but in all others the question is who can go fastest
in the road of amelioration. Railroads are already
projected on every side. Thirty public journals
(not political ones) are published where one was
before thought sufficient. Public meetings, dinners,
speeches, are taking place daily. Schools are instituted on every side. A new code of laws is on
the eve of being promulged, and the courts of
justice are for the first time thrown open. In fact,
where stagnation lately reigned, every thing is now
animation and activity."

"Rome, Dec. 17, 1846.

"Our dear friend M. has unexpectedly lost his
father, and is in great distress about it, having been
so much his companion and friend. I often think
that it is a merciful Providence that has been of

late teaching *us* to live asunder, and has thus been preparing us for a more lasting separation. I have of late been amusing myself with rhyming again; versifying a little fairy tale, over which I canter along with little or no effort. It is silly work, perhaps, but it suits my present powers, and gives me a little light occupation and amusement. I shall send M. a specimen, she being my great poetical correspondent, and her admiration of all my trash deserves this attention. . . . .

"It is curious to see how narrow and personal they all become, who have once conformed to Romanism. Is it a consciousness of the badness of their cause that induces them always to adopt this line of argument? Ventura told his audience the other day, that the author of the Anglican schism was Henry VIII.; and what, he asked, was to be expected from a man that had eighteen wives, and cut the heads off every one of them? Poor N. has got into sad disgrace here by the personalities with which *he* adorned his first public address. The Pope is much displeased, and says it is not 'Aceto' but 'Miele' that is suitable to such discourses."

"Rome, Jan. 8, 1847.

"I could tell you much about the worthy Pope here, who is vigorously pushing on his reforms. He has displaced the Governor of Rome, and of three of the provinces, for malpractices, and appointed others with clean hands in their stead. I went into the police-office to-day, and missing a very magisterial gentleman, that used to preside there, I was told that he and seven others had received their *mittimus.* The whole population of Rome, headed by the nobles, assembled on New Year's Day under the Pope's windows to salute him and ask his blessing, and I have little doubt that he may be called at this moment the most liberal and popular monarch in Europe. His encyclical letter lately published, though rather rabid against Bible societies, tract societies, socialism, rationalism, &c. is still full of excellent advice to the bishops and clergy of the Roman Church; and if his plans for general education, &c. are carried out, I cannot but anticipate great and happy changes in the moral aspect of this country. . . .

"We have a great deal too much of controversy here, without my courting more from across the water. It is an unhealthy atmosphere for my soul to breathe, and especially unsuitable to one that should be in hourly preparation for eternity. O that He who has all hearts at his disposal may raise mine daily above it, into that calm, clear, elevated region, where He is Himself seen and conversed with by faith, and where the soul may best ripen for his eternal presence and enjoyment."

"Rome, Jan. 26, 1847.

"You know what a round of stimulants is constantly kept up here, in order, as it were, to leave people no time for quiet thought. Well, all these I am obliged to forswear; and it is perhaps just as well that I should; for I am sure that the unceasing round of ceremonies, and processions, and masses, and sermons, is very like brandy-drinking, that keeps people in a state of intoxication, and unfits them for digesting wholesome food. A great deal, however, of quiet enjoyment is still open to me, and I have, at times, for days together, found myself so very well, so exempt from pain, from lassitude, from difficulty of breathing,—eating so heartily, sleeping so soundly, and exhibiting all the marks of health and vigour, that I am more than ever convinced that Mr. S. was right, when he said that my lungs were on the whole still perfectly sound, and all my complaints curable. . . . .

"Indeed, some of my visitors still continue their calls; among the rest dear M., who seldom lets a day slip by without our meeting. Indeed, we are almost the only two Anglicans left here, all the others having dropped down some pegs towards Evangelicalism, or having gone on into Romanism; so that, remaining, like the last roses of summer, we are obliged to strengthen each other's hands a little. He goes about a good deal, as usual, to hear the

sermons, and witness the ceremonies, and then
comes and takes a cup of tea with me in the evenings, when we talk matters over. I feel his conversation, indeed, more congenial than that of any one
else, though I fear we are sometimes provoked by
the intolerance and presumption of the .Church of
Rome, to lean more hardly on her than either of us
in our hearts are inclined to do. But really these
new converts to Romanism are so overbearing, and
so indefatigable in their efforts to effect new conversions, that they are quite intolerable. They
never allow one to be five minutes in their company
without giving the conversation a controversial
turn; and such an atmosphere is any thing but an
agreeable or a wholesome one for the soul to live
in. It is not pleasant to be obliged to live continually with one's armour on, and one's spear in
its rest; to be obliged to watch one's words, lest
you should make any admission that might be afterwards used against you, or allow your adversary to
establish a position from which he may afterwards·
advantageously assail you. To give you an instance
of this: I was introduced yesterday to Mrs. A.,
who, with her sisters, has conformed to Romanism,
and, after a few common places, she began to re-
mark on the beauty of seeing the common people
here so devout, and the contrast it furnished to
England in this respect. I questioned, however, the

fact of their being, as a body, more really devout than our English poor. She observed that there might be a few devout people amongst the dissenters, but that I had no right to take them into consideration. This point again I denied, urging that when she spoke of the Italian poor nationally, so she should speak of the English poor likewise as a body. She then asserted that the poor of the Church of England were unable to understand her Liturgy, full as it was of obsolete expressions, and involved sentences,—a point I again questioned, saying, that this diction, which she called obsolete, was the good old Saxon that still lingered in the phraseology of the peasantry,— but, however, that I thought an objection to the unintelligibility of the English Liturgy came with rather a bad grace from those whose sacred services were all carried on in Latin. O, but, she said, the people understand the Latin of the mass from their infancy ; and, had I ever remarked their devoutness when attending it ? I answered, that I had observed them sometimes apparently very devout; but, when I came to look more closely, I found that, instead of giving any attention to the mass that was celebrated in their presence, they had each their own little book of private devotions, on which all their thoughts and feelings seemed to be employed, to the neglect and disparagement of the holy rite which was then celebrated before them. Here was, I said, according to *their* views, the Great Sacrifice of Calvary renewed in their presence; here was the Lord of lords bodily appearing among them; and they, instead of being awed and absorbed by such a consideration, were occupying themselves with something else, which, however excellent it might be in itself, was a miserable and insulting intrusion when allowed to come between Him and them, between the Creator and his creatures. And this is the kind of running fight which one is obliged constantly to carry on here, not at all, in my mind, to the advancement of comfort or piety.

"Sometimes, indeed, we are provoked to carry the war a little into the enemy's camp. I think I said something in my last of a little skirmish we have lately had with some of the champions here, which, indeed, is not yet closed. M. had been to hear one of Ventura's sermons, and as he built a great deal on the text, M. turned to his little Bible to look at it. It was said by Ventura to be from the third of Malachi, 'Ecce advenit Dominator Dominus, &c.' 'Behold He cometh, the Lord, the Ruler! and in His hand, power, kingdom, and authority.' But, to M.'s surprise, he could find nothing of the kind there. On his return home he came to me, and asked me to show him the Vulgate; but, lo! there was no text like it there either. While we were at tea, as good luck would have it, Dr. Grant came in, so we referred the matter to him; but his endeavours to find the passage were as vain as our own. From him, however, we learned that the sentence occurred in the Introit for the day (the Epiphany) in the missal, and that it was there stated to be from Mal. iii.

"But now arose a more serious question, not as to the incorrectness of Father Ventura, but of the infallible missal itself. Had *it* quoted the passage incorrectly, and had it so stood for centuries, unnoticed by the missal's commentators or its ministers? Was the Bible so little known, or referred to, in the Church of Rome, that an error of this kind could remain so long undiscovered and uncorrected in the most distinguished of its formularies? The little doctor felt the importance of the point, and has been ever since endeavouring to explain the matter. His first solution was a very lame one. The introits, he said, were not all taken from Scripture, but many of them from the Fathers; and this, perhaps, was one of these. I begged him, however, to inform me which of the eminent fathers there was whose name began with 'Mal,' and what Mal. 'iii.' could possibly mean in this point of view. Finding, then, that this would not do, they referred the matter to N., I suppose as having been more recently conversant with Scrip-

ture than others among them; and his suggestion
was, that the passage was taken, not from the Vulgate, but the old Italic version. However, this has, I
suppose, likewise failed them; for, yesterday, M. received a note from Dr. G., saying that he believed
the passage not to be a quotation from Scripture at
all, but a 'paraphrase' of the whole chapter in
question; to which M. has replied that the solution
of the difficulty was by no means satisfactory, more
especially as a paraphrase was generally understood
to be an explanation in a fuller form, and the
words in question had any thing but that character
about them. *I* contented myself with merely asking
the Dr. this morning, when I met him for a moment,
whether this was the way in which his Church
usually dealt with Scripture, giving the people *her
own* words, and referring to *them* as the Word of
God? I dare say we shall hear something more
about the matter, as we do not intend to let it drop
here. Having put such a hook in Leviathan, it
would be a pity not to play him a little."

"Rome, Feb. 6, 1847.

"We have several different classes of visitors,—
a very large section are mere pleasure-hunters,
whose carriages I hear, night after night, rolling
over the pavement to their various balls and parties.
Another class are the sight-seers, with their necks

and eyes ever on the stretch. These swallow much intellectual food and digest little, so that they are, many of them, little better than walking hand-books. Another considerable class here are the converts, very few of them persons of much mental power, but possessing all the zeal for which people of this class, to whatever sect they belong, are famous. They wear rose-coloured spectacles, through which they view all the fooleries and enormities of the papal system, and are very anxious to transfer them from their own noses to those of other people. . . . .

" The Pope, in whom you rightly take such an interest, stole down the other day, at three in the afternoon, to the Church of St. Andrew della Valle, and, taking the pulpit, instead of the ordinary preacher, gave the poor people a most earnest extempore sermon. He spoke strongly against habitual blasphemy, against pride of dress, and other vanities of Rome; and after his sermon, prayed, also extempore, for a considerable time. After this he buried his face in his hands in the deepest emotion, and continued absorbed in private prayer, so much so as to forget to give the customary benediction, which was given by a cardinal present instead. It is more than a century since any other pontiff has preached. Scarcely a day passes without our hearing of some of his good deeds. He has given more than 400*l.* out of his narrow income (not 25,000*l.* a year) for the poor Irish. The night before last he went, after night fall, to the house of a poor widow here to examine into her circumstances and relieve her. . . . .

"The Carnival is just commenced here with very inauspicious weather,—cold, wet, stormy, cloudy;—every thing but that which suits us poor invalids. But we have what God thinks best for us; and if He comes with it, all must be well."

" Feb. 16, 1847.

" The people round, too, have been most kind in their offers and inquiries, especially dear M., who has seen me once, and often twice a day, throughout my illness. He administered the Holy Communion to P. and me yesterday, and has been of the greatest comfort to me. The Carnival, in the mean time, has been going on here, and disturbing us poor invalids by its nocturnal revels, or rather, by the carriages rolling past us to partake of them. However, to-day will see its termination. Indeed, while I am writing this, ' Il Carnivale è morto,' and the maskers are preparing to pass from comedy to tragedy, from the Carnival to Lent, and we shall at least have quiet for a few weeks. Very irreverent talking all this, you will say; but, really, the more I am ac-quainted with the religion of this land, the more

unreal do I think it, and the more do I feel it to
consist in mere externals. With the exception of
the new English converts, who have been brought
up in a different school, and a few select others, I
cannot help feeling that I am living among actors,
and that if old Juvenal got up again from his grave,
he would not err much in singing, as he did of old,
'Natio comœda est.' The most agreeable object to
dwell on, in connexion with the Church of Rome,
is the man that is at the head of it. He is certainly a very fine fellow. I mentioned, in my last
letter to M., how he had been preaching and praying
here. I have just heard of another of his noble
acts that is equally striking. Bouchon, the French
preacher, has been narrating it. He sent, yesterday,
for all the Lent preachers of Rome, one hundred
and forty in number, to the Quirinal palace. They
assembled in an antechamber, and the Pope sent
them word, before they came into his presence, to
go through an act of faith; on which they all repeated aloud the Creed (that, I presume, of Pope
Pius). They were then ushered into the audience-
room, when the Pope addressed them on their
duties during the approaching season for an hour
and a half, not only, as Bouchon said, most wisely,
but in a nobler strain of real eloquence than he had
ever heard from any other lips. He (the Pope)
shed tears more than once in the delivery of his

address, and at the close made them all kneel down with him, and offered up a most touching and impressive prayer for them and for himself. One really feels that this man must be in earnest, and that God's blessing must descend on such efforts. In what shape, indeed, may be dubious; whether in the way of advancement to the Church of Rome as she now stands, or in the substitution of something better, may admit of a question."

" Rome, March 15, 1847.

" With regard to this old city, I have not, I fear, much in the way of news to give you. We are all very quiet here at this season; no balls, no plays, no noisy parties, except among some of our graceless English. The Romans are all busy in attending their religious services during Lent. There are sermons in almost all of the churches daily. A large number of persons are likewise, at this time, in what they call 'a Retreat.' One of the great convents here is opened for the reception of persons wishing to engage in these religious exercises. Those who enter are lodged in separate rooms, or cells, and hold no communication with each other. Thrice a day they attend public worship, and hear addresses on religious subjects (generally forming a regular course), and spend the rest of their time in religious reading, meditation, and prayer. This lasts generally for ten days or a fortnight (and there are twenty or thirty going on at the same time), and appears to produce the very best effects on those that attend, in many instances appearing to work a true and lasting conversion. There is another curious service that now takes place in the churches, the 'Missioni.' It is a kind of improvement on catechetical lecturing, and is intended specially for the lower orders, though very popular among all ranks. The last that I witnessed was carried on by two Jesuits, in St. Andrew, an immense church, which was crowded on the occasion from end to end. About the middle of the church was a platform erected, and after Divine service the two performers got up on this stage, and took their seats. One of them personated the 'Ignorante,' or common people, and the other his instructor, and the latter began by asking the former if he remembered any thing of his last lesson; to which the other replied that he did, and recapitulated some part of it. 'But,' said he, 'it is really of very little use that we should go on with these lessons, for I have just heard of a very formidable conspiracy, that is now hatching in Rome, and that will go far to upset the existing order of things.' 'Pooh, pooh, my dear fellow,' replied the instructor, 'don't talk of conspiracies in these days; the time for conspiracies

g

is over now; and besides, under our present good Pope'— 'Ah, my friend,' interrupted the ignorante, here is the worst feature in the business:—I very much fear that the Pope himself is at the bottom of it. Do you know that I heard one of the conspirators say that the Pope was decidedly encouraging their designs.' At last it comes out that this conspiracy is a kind of pledge which certain persons were taking against swearing, in consequence of a sermon preached by the Pope against this vice. And in this strain the conversation between the ignorante and his instructor went on for more than an hour, the most excellent instruction being conveyed in the most graphic and amusing manner. One cannot help wishing that a Church, which has so many wise and effective modes of teaching, and such admirable institutions, had something better than mere formalities to convey by means of them."

" Rome, Spring of 1847.

"But you are dying, I know, to hear something more about that fine fellow the Pope. Well, among his reforms, one is, that he has dismissed more than half of the beggars of Rome. They come most of them from Naples, and the Pope sends round every few days, picks them all up, and simply carts them to the frontier, and then drops them within their own territory. One of the blind men accordingly, that clinked the little porringers on the top of the Pincian steps in your ears, is vanished. Another, who used to thrust a fin, or pinion, in your face, near the French academy, does so no more. The poor Pope, however, has, we hear, a hard task of it. A conspiracy against him has just been detected at Ancona, in which many of the Frate Dominicane have been engaged. They had collected the sinews of war to the amount of 25,000 scudi; but the governor pounced on their treasure and correspondence, and seven of them have reached the castle of St. Angelo. They say the Pope is intent on reforming the Irish clergy, and means to make the monasteries here rather retreats for the aged, than resting-places for the young and lazy. He is going to make a grand reform in the sacred music of the Church, so as to make it more uniform, and less theatrical. He has accordingly set on foot a commission who are to consult all the old scores of sacred music, and make a grand selection from them, to the discarding of modern flourishes, and with a special eye to the revival of the old Gregorian chant."

"Rome, March 16, 1847.

" I must not touch on religious matters at such a part of my letter, though there is much that I could wish to say. I think most of the Anglicans here have passed through that dangerous period, when, dissatisfied with the state of things at home, they look elsewhere, and find all *couleur de rose* in the Church of Rome, till a closer inspection does away with the delusion, and makes them feel, with Hamlet, that it is better 'to bear the ills we have, than fly to others that we know not of.' "

" Rome, March 27, 1847.

"And now what shall I tell you of old Rome, its inhabitants, and their doings ? All is very quiet here just now during Lent. Balls and noisy parties are given up by all but a few graceless English. The only thing of the kind that is tolerated is music, and this chiefly at charitable concerts. A grand amateur concert takes place this evening, for the poor Irish, in which Mrs. S. and Mrs. B. sing, and many likewise of the Italian nobility and gentry. The Pope has given 200*l.* more out of his small income to the Irish sufferers, and there is talk of his preaching himself in their behalf. A priest here has sold his library, a very fine one, and sent all the produce to the same quarter. Another person has given a picture worth 1000*l.*; so that there is no want of sympathy for the poor sufferers here. I only grieve to think that many of them show themselves so undeserving of the generosity that has been exhibited towards them."

"To-morrow will commence the ceremonies of the Holy Week here, in which I shall have little participation, though I should like, if possible, to hear one of the misereres. Certainly, nothing earthly that I know of comes up to it. The last that I heard, though I had, I thought, made up my mind to sit through it unmoved, yet the second note overcame me, and I fairly wept through the whole piece. There is no instrumental music on the occasion, but a single voice begins in a soft under-note, when another and another drops harmoniously in, the same note being still held on, till at length the whole united choir pour out all their strength and sweetness, the voices gradually dying away as they began. Such is the *first note* of the miserere, which alone occupies a minute or two. As to many of the other ceremonies of the Holy Week they are, in my estimation, miserably offensive, and many of them absolutely ludicrous. I dare say the present Pontiff will give them as much dignity as any one could ; but it is impossible to make them tolerable to a person of any good taste, not to say piety."

"Rome, April 7, 1847.

"The Pope has been as usual pouring out his bounty on the poor here. He has provided every poor family in the city with bread for three days,

and given 3000 scudi amongst them. No wonder
that he should be so adored. To-day all the English
converts have gone in a body to be presented to
him. Their number here is seventy-nine. Ventura, however, who counts by wholesale, told the
people in a sermon of his yesterday, that in England
they only heard of a few of the principal converts,
but that really whole districts and counties had become Roman Catholic. In one city alone in England, he said, where a short time since there were
only three or four Catholics, there are now 70,000 :
and the people here swallow all this exaggerated
stuff as Gospel.

"There are, however, others as well as he, very
ill satisfied with what they find in the Romish
Church now that they have joined it. Little Mr.
H., I am told, speaks very freely of the need of
reform in her communion; and even R. is not, I
think, quite at ease. Indeed it can hardly be otherwise than that they should meet with many disap-
pointments, in the reckless way in which they have
been pushing their conversions. They care not
whether a man is convinced or not, but press him
to join them, with all his objections, and expect
them all in due time to vanish. This is very hand-
over-head work, and will have its reward by-and-
by.'

" Berry-Head, Aug. 25, 1847.

" MY DEAR FRIEND,

" *You* used to be the diligent correspondent, and
I the remiss one,—and so ought it to be now, for
to you writing is a pleasure, and to me a toil and a
distress,—and yet you are two letters in my debt,
and I write again to ask you to give me a *screed* of
your heart and mind, before seas again roar between
us. I am meditating flight again to the south.
The little faithful robin is every morning at my
window, sweetly warning me that autumnal hours
are at hand. The swallows are preparing for flight,
and inviting me to accompany them, and yet, alas!
while I talk of flying, I am just able to crawl, and
often ask myself whether I shall be able to leave
England at all.   .   .   .   .   But you know how the
spring rises with me as soon as the pressure is removed. I am, therefore, calculating, with many a
Deo Volente, on taking up my staff in rather less
than three weeks from the present time. I. and E.
will be my *compagnons de voyage*, together with
faithful, indefatigable P., and we shall probably go
direct through France to Marseilles, and from
thence to Naples. I must of course look for many
restings by the way; but, if we can get to the
south of France early in October, I shall hope to
do well. The autumns are always severe north of
Lyons, and the Alps generally snow-clad early in

September. At Naples, we should probably pause
for a few weeks, and then proceed to Palermo, where
the fields generally continue in flower till Christmas.
There I should like to remain till February, when
we might, if all are spared, return to Italy again,
and get up to Rome for the spring season. Such
is a sketch of my plans. How small a part of
them may we be permitted to carry into exe-
cution! and yet it is right to form them, while
we leave the rest to Him who does for us better
than we could for ourselves. O for more of entire
dependence on Him! entire confidence in Him!
Not, I hope, that I am quite without these, but I
want to feel them more a living principle of action.
Conformity to the will and image of the Lord is no
easy attainment, and it takes much hammering to
bend us to it."

                              " Avignon, Oct. 19, 1847.

" Again I sit down to pen a few lines to you, and to
tell you that we are all pretty well. . . My intention, now that I have at length reached these milder
regions, is to loiter here awhile, and after visiting
Nismes, Montpellier, Arles, and other objects of
interest in the neighbourhood, to move on to Nice,
at the Poste Restaute of which I trust we shall find
letters to rejoice our hearts. . . I hear glowing
accounts indeed of Nice itself for winter-quarters,
especially for persons suffering from bronchial com-

plaints. However, a few days' residence there will tell me more of its suitability to me than any thing I can learn from the reports of others.

"More, however, of these matters when I write from Nice. In the mean time we shall be longing for news from home; and let your letters be in imitation of mine as far as egotism is concerned, for you cannot tell me too much of yourself and all around you."

"La Pallise, Oct. 10, 1847.

"I write from a little town scarcely mentioned in maps, where we are spending our Sunday. It lies between Moulins and Roanne, a quiet place, with a tolerable little inn and civil landlady, with a tidy little daughter, all great attractions to poor, jaded, cheated travellers like ourselves. . . .

"The autumn is evidently much more advanced here than in England. Many of the trees have lost their leaves altogether; and those that retain them exhibit a variety and brilliancy of autumnal colouring—yellow, orange, red, purple, and green,—unknown in England. I never saw any thing more exquisite than the woodland scenery we passed through yesterday. The country was tame and flat enough in itself, but the trees, with their hundred hues, clothed it in inexpressible beauty. Still I shall not be sorry to take my leave of them. Scenery can be ill enjoyed when it is a labour to fetch one breath after another.

I am therefore looking on anxiously to the Rhone, which is to hurry us down a hundred miles to the south in the course of one forenoon. . . . .

"Thence to Avignon is a morning's excursion; and there we shall probably rest three or four days or more, exploring afterwards Nismes, Arles, and Aix, and so beating our way to Nice, or Nizza, as it is called by the Italians. From Aix thither will be a three days' journey, and Nice is therefore the place at which we can next hope to hear from you, unless indeed your kind sagacity may have addressed a letter for me to Lyons or Avignon."

"Avignon, Oct. 20, 1847.

"You have perhaps ere now been expecting a line from me, but I have been unable to write before. I have, ever since I saw you, been either travelling or in bed." . . . .

"Ever since we have been creeping forward by slow stages, hitherto, over cold, cheerless, uninteresting, France; and the day before yesterday reached the valley of the Rhone, where the climate became entirely changed, and I began to breathe and move again freely in the warm atmosphere of Provence. It is quite surprising how much warmer it is in this favoured region. The thermometer stands at 68°: we have no longer any need of fires. Fresh fruits of all kinds abound, and the bunches of grapes rival those of Eshcol. The scenery in this valley also is pre-eminently beautiful. It is the Rhine on a larger scale: the mountains, as you pass down the river Rhone, assume the most picturesque aspects. Sometimes they close in on the stream, and again recede into the blue distance, out-topped occasionally by the remoter snowy Alps. The banks of the river itself are clothed all the way down with vineyards, producing some of the finest wines in France, Hermitage, Frontignac, &c. But the most striking objects of all are the woods, which present a variety and richness of hues—yellow, orange, crimson, purple, and green—unknown in the landscapes of our English autumns. The colours are so vivid, that if they were faithfully set down on canvass, an English eye must pronounce them unnatural—so true it is that what art dares not attempt, nature does.

"But to return to personals. I am truly thankful for the little interview I had with you, almost beyond expectation, before my departure. Though I said little, I felt much, and carried away impressions that will remain with me till we meet again. Where that meeting will be, He that ordereth all things alone knows: yet, after so many meetings and partings as we have experienced on earth, perhaps it may be even in this world. . . . . What our future movements will be, is scarcely yet decided;

but we shall, I think, now that we have reached a more genial climate, linger here a little. There is much to interest in the shape of Roman antiquities at Nismes and Arles; and after visiting them we shall, I think, move on to Nice and Genoa, and be guided in our further progress by the reports we hear from Italy. I shall, I trust, find a letter from you at Nice."

" Commenced at Arles, finished at Aix,
Nov. 3, 1847.

" I hope you have not been very anxious to hear of us or from us, though you will, I dare say, be surprised at hearing from this place. We are, however, pursuant to our plan before leaving England, continuing to loiter here in the south of France. . . . .

" On Thursday we hope to be at Nice, and to remain there at least a week. I have already sent to bespeak apartments, through a gentleman whose acquaintance I made at Avignon. . . . .

" It will be no small treat also to hear at length from home again: we are absolutely thirsting for news of you all; trusting, indeed, that the same merciful Father is protecting you who is protecting us, but longing to know this for certain. I have myself been wonderfully well for the last ten days, though the weather has been by no means warm." . . . .

Poems.

POEMS.

 FRIENDS LOST IN 1833.

Gone?—Have ye all then gone,—
The good, the beautiful, the kind, the dear?
Passed to your glorious rest so swiftly on,
    And left me weeping here?

I gaze on your bright track;
I hear your lessening voices as ye go.
Have ye no sign, no solace, to fling back
    To us who toil below?

They hear not my faint cry;
Beyond the range of sense for ever flown,
I see them melt into eternity,
    And feel I am alone.

Into the haven pass'd,
They anchor far beyond the scathe of ill;
While the stern billow, and the reckless blast
    Are mine to cope with still.

Oh! from that land of love,
Look ye not sometimes on this world of woe?
Think you not, dear ones, in bright bowers above,
    Of those you've left below?

Surely ye note us here,
Though not as we appear to mortal view;
And can we still, with all our stains, be dear
    To spirits pure as you?

Do ye not loathe,—not spurn,—
The worms of clay, the slaves of sense and will ?
When ye from God and glory earthward turn,
    Oh! can ye love us still ?

Or, have ye rather now
Drunk of His Spirit whom ye worship there,
Who stripp'd the crown of glory from His brow,
    The platted thorns to wear ?

Is it a fair fond thought,
That you may still our friends and guardians be,
And Heaven's high ministry by you be wrought
    With abjects low as we ?

May we not sweetly hope
That you around our path and bed may dwell ?
And shall not all our blessings brighter drop
    From hands we loved so well ?

Shall we not feel you near
In hours of danger, solitude, and pain,
Cheering the darkness, drying off the tear,
    And turning loss to gain ?

Shall not your gentle voice
Break on temptation's dark and sullen mood,
Subdue our erring will, o'errule our choice,
    And win from ill to good ?

O yes ! to us, to us,
A portion of your converse still be given :
Struggling affection still would hold you thus,
    Nor yield you all to Heaven!

Lead our faint steps to God ;
Be with us while the desert here we roam ;
Teach us to tread the path which you have trod,
    To find with you our home !

STANZAS TO J. K.

WHAT strains are these, what sweet familiar num-
    bers,
From old Ierne o'er the waters wend?   [bers,
How welcome, wakening from its lengthen'd slum-
    Sounds the heart-music of my earliest Friend!
Well might that hand amid the chords have falter'd,
    That voice have lost the power to melt and move:
How pleasant, then, to find them still unalter'd,
    That lyre in sweetness, and that heart in love!

Shall not my tuneful powers, too long neglected,
    Revive to answer that persuasive call?—
Like the old harp that, mould'ring and rejected,
    Hangs up in silence in some lonely hall,
When youth and beauty's train there re-assembles,
    And mirth and song once more begin to flow,

Light o'er the chords a mimic music trembles,
  Responsive to the notes that swell below!

Ah me!—what thoughts those few bold notes a-
      waken,—
  Bright recollections of life's morning hours;
Haunts long remembered, and too soon forsaken;
  Days that fled by in sunshine, song, and flowers;
Old Clogher's rocks, our own sequester'd valley;
  Wild walks by moonlight on the sounding shore,
Hearts warm and free, light laugh, and playful
      sally,
  All that has been,—and shall return no more—

No more,—no more,—moods ever new and changing,
  Feelings that forth in song so freely gush'd,
Wing'd hopes, high fancies, thoughts unfetter'd
      ranging—
  Flowers which the world's cold ploughshare
      since has crush'd.

Dear early visions of departed gladness,
   Ye rise, ye live a moment in that strain,
A gleam of sunshine on life's wintry sadness,
   Ah! why so bright, to flit so soon again?

Friend of my heart!—since those young visions
      perish'd,
   We've trod a chequer'd path of good and ill;
We've seen the wreck of much that once we cherish'd,
   But not the wreck of love and friendship still.
No, hand in hand we've met life's stormy weather,
   Sustain'd the buffetings of foe and friend,
And hand in hand and heart in heart together,
   We'll help and cheer each other to the end.

Strike then the chords!—alas, too rarely stricken,
   And I will answer in my humbler style:
No voice like thine can soothe, can urge, can
      quicken,—
   Why has it been so little heard ere while?

Yes, strike the chords! high thoughts and aims
   inspiring;
And up the narrow way we'll homeward move,
Mingling our pilgrim songs, and here acquiring
 New hearts and voices for the songs above.

Berryhead, 1840.

SEA CHANGES.

From shore to shore the waters sleep,
   Without a breath to move them;
And mirror many a fathom deep
   Rocks round and skies above them.
I catch the sea-bird's lightest wail
   That dots the distant billow,
And hear the flappings of the sail
   That lull the sea-boy's pillow.

Anon—across the glassy bay
   The catspaw gusts come creeping;
A thousand waves are soon at play,
   In sunny freshness leaping.

The surge once more talks round the shore,
   The good ship walks the ocean;
Seas, skies, and men all wake again
   To music, health, and motion.

But now the clouds, in angry crowds,
   On Heaven's grim forehead muster,
And wild and wide sweeps o'er the tide
   The white squall's fitful bluster.
The stout ship heels, the brave heart reels
   Before the 'whelming breaker;
And all in nature quakes, and feels
   The presence of its Maker.

Oh, glorious still in every form,
   Untamed, untrodden ocean;
Beneath the sunshine, or the storm,
   In stillness, or commotion;

Be mine to dwell beside the swell,
　　A witness of thy wonders;
Feel thy light spray around me play,
　　And thrill before thy thunders!

While yet a boy I felt it joy
　　To gaze upon thy glories;
I loved to ride thy stormy tide,
　　And shout in joyous chorus.
With calmer brow I haunt thee now,
　　To nurse sublime emotion;
My soul is awed, and fill'd with God,
　　By thee, majestic ocean!

1840.

DAVID'S THREE MIGHTY ONES.

"And David longed, and said, Oh that one would give me drink of the water of the well of Bethlehem, which is by the gate!"—2 SAM. xxiii. 15.

FAINT on Rephaim's sultry side
    Sat Israel's warrior king;
" Oh for one draught," the hero cried,
    " From Bethlehem's cooling spring!—
From Bethlehem's spring, upon whose brink
My youthful knee bent down to drink!

" I know the spot, by yonder gate,
    Beside my father's home,
Where pilgrims love at eve to wait,
    And girls for water come.
Oh for that healing water now,
To quench my lip, to cool my brow!

" But round that gate, and in that home,
   And by that sacred well,
Now hostile feet insulting roam,
   And impious voices swell.
The Philistine holds Bethlehem's halls,
While we pine here beneath its walls."—

Three gallant men stood nigh, and heard
   The wish their king expressed;
Exchanged a glance, but not a word,
   And dash'd from 'midst the rest.
And strong in zeal, with ardour flushed,
They up the hill to Bethlehem rushed.

The foe fast mustering to attack,
   Their fierceness could not rein;
No friendly voice could call them back.—
   " Shall David long in vain ?
" Long for a cup from Bethlehem's spring,
" And none attempt the boon to bring ?"

And now the city gate they gain,
    And now in conflict close;
Unequal odds! three dauntless men
    Against unnumbered foes.
Yet through their ranks they plough their way
Like galleys through the ocean spray.

The gate is forced, the crowd is pass'd;
    They scour the open street;
While hosts are gathering fierce and fast
    To block up their retreat.
Haste back! haste back, ye desperate Three!
Or Bethlehem soon your grave must be!

They come again;—and with them bring—
    Nor gems nor golden prey;
A single cup from Bethlehem's spring
    Is all they bear away;
And through the densest of the train
Fight back their glorious way again.

O'er broken shields and prostrate foes
   They urge their conquering course.
Go, try the tempest to oppose,
   Arrest the lightning's force;
But hope not, Pagans, to withstand
The shock of Israel's chosen band!

Hurrah! hurrah! again they're free;
   And 'neath the open sky,
On the green turf they bend the knee,
   And lift the prize on high;
Then onward through the shouting throng
To David bear their spoil along.

All in their blood and dust they sink
   Full low before their king.
" Again," they cry, " let David drink
   Of his own silver spring;
And if the draught our lord delight,
His servants' toil 'twill well requite."

With deep emotion David took
    From their red hands the cup;
Cast on its stains a shuddering look,
    And held it heavenward up.
" I prize your boon," exclaimed the king,
" But dare not taste the draught you bring.

" I prize the zeal that perill'd life,
    A wish of mine to crown;
I prize the might that in the strife
    Bore foes by thousands down :—
But dare not please myself with aught
By Israel's blood and peril bought.

" To Heaven the glorious spoil is due;
    And His the offering be,
Whose arm has borne you safely through,
    My brave, but reckless, Three!"—
Then on the earth the cup he pour'd,
A free libation to the Lord.

There is a well in Bethlehem still,
　　A fountain, at whose brink
The weary soul may rest at will,
　　The thirsty stoop and drink:
And unrepelled by foe or fence
Draw living waters freely thence.

Oh, did we thirst as David then
　　For this diviner spring!
Had we the zeal of David's men
　　To please a Higher King!
What precious draughts we thence might drain,
What holy triumphs daily gain!

A RECALL TO MY CHILD A. M.

JUNE 1, 1839.

COME back, come back, my blessed child!
  Come home, my own light hearted!
Papa, they say, has rarely smiled
  Since from his side you parted.—
That face which beams like opening day,
  That laugh which never wearies;
Why do they linger still away?
  Come home, dear girl, and cheer us!

I saunter sadly through my hours,—
  They want one voice to mend them;
A spell is o'er my drooping flowers,—
  They pine for you to tend them.

The fairest now look all amiss,
　　Too dingy, or too flaunting.—
And are they changed? ah, no, 'tis this—
　　The sweetest flower is wanting!

Young spring at last, despite the shocks
　　Of winter's lingering bluster,
Has flung her mantle o'er our rocks,
　　And clothed our hills with lustre.
Music, and balm, and beauty play
　　In all around and o'er us.
" Come, truant, come," all seem to say:
　　" Come, join our happy chorus."

" Come," cries the cowslip's fading bell;
　　" Come," cries the ripening cherry;
" Come, ere the bloom in every dell
　　Is turn'd to pod and berry;

c 2

Come, ere the cuckoo change his tone;
   Ere from her nest the linnet,
With all her little ones, is flown,
   And you've ne'er peep'd within it."

The sun sets not so brightly now,
   Across the golden water,
As when it gleam'd upon the brow
   Of my loved absent daughter.
Home has no more its cheerful tone,
   Its healthful hue about it:—
When from the lyre one chord is gone
   The rest sound ill without it.

Come back; the city's flaunting crowd,
   The concert's formal measures,
The din of fashion, false and loud,
   Are not like nature's pleasures.—

These, these alone, the heart can touch,
  Are simplest and sincerest.
You have an eye, a soul for such :
  Come home, and share them, dearest.

Come, at my side, again to walk
  Beside the fresh'ning billow.
Come, where the waves all night will talk
  To you upon your pillow.
Come, where the skiff on sunny seas
  For you is lightly riding ;
Where health and song in ev'ry breeze
  My absent girl come chiding.

Come back ! we all from your glad eyes
  New light and life will borrow.
'Tis not papa alone that sighs,
  " Why leave me to my sorrow ? "

Each, all in your loved converse miss
    Some wonted source of pleasure,
From look, or tone, or smile, or kiss :
    Come home, come home, my treasure!

DECLINING DAYS.

" Quod in vita est optanda sapienti, profecto nullam aliam
ob causam vivere optaverim, quam ut aliquid efficiam, quod
vita dignum sit; et quod utilitatem legentibus, etsi non ad elo-
quentiam, quia tenuis in nobis eloquentiæ rivus est, ad vivendum
tamen adferat, quod est maxime necessarium. Quo profecto,
satis me vixisse arbitrabor, et officium hominis implesse, si
labor meus aliquos homines ab erroribus liberatos, ad iter cœ-
leste direxerit."—LACTANTIUS, *De Opif. Dei*, cap. xx.

·WHY do I sigh to find
Life's evening shadows gathering round my way?
The keen eye dimming, and the buoyant mind
    Unhinging day by day?

    Is it the natural dread
Of that stern lot, which all who live must see?
The worm, the clay, the dark and narrow bed,—
    Have these such awe for me?

Can I not summon pride
To fold my decent mantle round my breast;
And lay me down at nature's Eventide,
 Calm to my dreamless rest?

As nears my soul the verge
Of this dim continent of woe and crime,
Shrinks she to hear Eternity's long surge
 Break on the shores of Time?

Asks she, how she shall fare
When conscience stands before the Judge's throne,
And gives her record in, and all shall there
 Know, as they all are known?

A solemn scene and time—
And well may Nature quail to feel them near—
But grace in feeble breasts can work sublime,
 And faith o'ermaster fear!

Hark ! from that throne comes down
A voice which strength to sinking souls can give,
That voice all Judgment's thunders cannot drown ;
    " Believe," it cries, " and live."

Weak—sinful, as I am,
That still small voice forbids me to despond ;
Faith clings for refuge to the bleeding Lamb,
    Nor dreads the gloom beyond.—

'Tis not then earth's delights
From which my spirit feels so loath to part ;
Not the dim future's solemn sounds or sights
    That press so on my heart.

No! 'tis the thought that I—
My lamp so low, my sun so nearly set,
Have lived so useless, so unmiss'd should die :—
    'Tis this, I now regret.—

I would not be the wave
That swells and ripples up to yonder shore;
That drives impulsive on, the wild wind's slave,
      And breaks, and is no more!—

I would not be the breeze,
That murmurs by me in its viewless play,
Bends the light grass, and flutters in the trees,
      And sighs and flits away!

No! not like wave or wind
Be my career across the earthly scene;
To come and go, and leave no trace behind
      To say that I have been.

I want not vulgar fame—
I seek not to survive in brass or stone;
Hearts may not kindle when they hear my name,
      Nor tears my value own.—

But might I leave behind
Some blessing for my fellows, some fair trust
To guide, to cheer, to elevate my kind
    When I was in the dust.

Within my narrow bed
Might I not wholly mute or useless be ;
But hope that they, who trampled o'er my head
    Drew still some good from me !

Might my poor lyre but give
Some simple strain, some spirit-moving lay ;
Some sparklet of the Soul, that still might live
    When I was passed to clay !

Might verse of mine inspire
One virtuous aim, one high resolve impart ;
Light in one drooping soul a hallow'd fire,
    Or bind one broken heart.

Death would be sweeter then,
More calm my slumber 'neath the silent sod ;
Might I thus live to bless my fellow men,
　　Or glorify my God !

Why do we ever lose
As judgment ripens our diviner powers ?
Why do we only learn our gifts to use
　　When they no more are ours ?

O Thou ! whose touch can lend
Life to the dead, Thy quick'ning grace supply,
And grant me, swanlike, my last breath to spend
　　In song that may not die !

THE DYING CHRISTIAN TO HIS SOUL.

Bird of my breast, away!
The long-wish'd hour is come!
On to the realms of cloudless day,
On to thy glorious home!

Long has been thine to mourn
In banishment and pain.
Return, thou wand'ring dove, return,
And find thy ark again!

Away, on joyous wing,
Immensity to range;
Around the throne to soar and sing,
And faith for sight exchange.

Lo! to the golden gate
What shining thousands come!
My trembling Soul, for thee they wait,
To guard and guide thee home.

Hark! from on high they speak,
That bright and blessed train,
"Rise, Heaven-born spirit, rise, and seek
Thy rest in Heaven gain.

"Sweet are the songs above,
Where hearts are all in tune;
They feed upon unfailing love,
And bask in glory's noon.

"Their struggles all are still,
Their days of darkness o'er;
At rapture's fount they drink at will,
And drink for evermore.

"Flee, then, from sin and woe,
  To joys immortal flee;
Quit thy dark prison-house below,
  And be for ever free!"

I come, ye blessed throng,
  Your tasks and joys to share;
O, fill my lips with holy song,
  My drooping wing upbear.

Friends of my heart, adieu!
  I cannot weep to-day.
The tears that nature prompts for you
  Are dried in glory's ray.

I see the King of kings,
  His glorious voice I hear.
O, who can dwell on earthly things
  With Heaven so bright and near?

NAPOLEON'S GRAVE.

*Addressed to the French nation on their proposing to remove
Napoleon's remains from St. Helena to France.*

DISTURB him not! he slumbers well
   On his rock 'mid the western deep,
Where the broad blue waters round him swell,
   And the tempests o'er him sweep.
O, leave him where his mountain bed
   Looks o'er the Atlantic wave,
And the mariner high in the far grey sky
   Points out Napoleon's grave!

There, 'midst three mighty continents
   That trembled at his word,
Wrapt in his shroud of airy cloud,
   Sleeps Europe's warrior lord:

And there, on the heights, still seems to stand,
   At eve, his shadowy form ;
His grey capote on the mist to float,
   And his voice in the midnight storm.

Disturb him not! though bleak and bare,
   That spot is all his own ;
And truer homage was paid him there
   Than on his hard-won throne.
Earth's trembling monarchs there at bay
   The cagèd lion kept ;
For they knew with dread that his iron tread
   Woke earthquakes where he stept.

Disturb him not! vain France, thy clime
   No resting-place supplies,
So meet, so glorious, so sublime,
   As that where thy Hero lies.

D

Mock not that grim and mouldering wreck!
  Revere that bleaching brow!
Nor call the dead from his grave to deck
  A puppet pageant now!

Born in a time when blood and crime
  Raged through thy realm at will,
He waved his hand o'er the troubled land,
  And the storm at once was still.
He reared from the dust thy prostrate state;
  Thy war-flag wide unfurl'd;
And bade thee thunder at every gate
  Of the capitals of the world.

And will ye from his rest dare call
  The thunderbolt of war!
To grin and chatter around his pall,
  And scream your " vive la gloire?"

Shall melo-dramic obsequies
　His honoured dust deride?
Forbid it, human sympathies!
　Forbid it, Gallic pride!

What! will no withering thought occur,
　No thrill of cold mistrust,
How empty all this pomp and stir
　Above a little dust?
And will it not your pageant dim,
　Your arrogance rebuke,
To see what now remains of him,
　Who once the empires shook?

Then let him rest in his stately couch
　Beneath the open sky,
Where the wild waves dash, and the lightnings
　　flash,
　And the storms go wailing by.

Yes, let him rest! such men as he
Are of no time or place;
They live for ages yet to be,
They die for all their race.

GRACE DARLING'S DEATH-BED.

O WIPE the death-dews from her brow!—prop up
    her sinking head!—
And let the sea-breeze on her face its welcome
    freshness shed!
She loves to see the western sun pour glory o'er
    the deep;
And the music of the rippling waves may sing her
    into sleep.
Her heart has long, 'mid other scenes, for these
    pour'd out the sigh;
And now back to her highland home she comes—
    but comes to die.

Yes, fearful in its loveliness, that cheek's prophetic
    bloom;
That lustrous eye is lighted from a world beyond
    the tomb;
Those thin transparent fingers, that hold the book
    of prayer,
That form, which melts like summer snow, too
    plainly speak despair.
And they that tend around her bed, oft turn to
    wipe the tear,
That starts forth, as they view her thus, so fleeting,
    and so dear.

Not such was she that awful night when o'er
    Northumbria's foam
The shipwreck'd seaman's cry was heard within
    that rocky home.
Amid the pauses of the storm it loud and louder
    came,

And thrilled into her inmost soul, and nerved her
    fragile frame.
" Oh, father, let us launch the boat, and try their
    lives to save."
" Be still, my child, we should but go to share their
    watery grave."

Again they shriek. " O father, come, the Lord our
    guide will be :
A word from Him can stay the blast, and tame the
    raging sea."
And lo ! at length her plea prevails ; their skiff is
    on the wave.
Protect them, gracious Heaven ; protect the gentle,
    kind, and brave.
They reach the rock, and, wond'rous sight to those
    they succour there,
A feeble girl achieving more than boldest men
    would dare !

Again, again her venturous bark bounds o'er the
    foaming tide ;
Again in safety goes and comes beneath its Heavenly
    guide.
Nor shrinks that maid's heroic heart, nor fails her
    willing hand,
'Till all the remnant of the wreck are ferried safe
    to land.
The cord o'erstrung relaxes then, and tears begin
    to fall ;—
But tears of love and praise to Him, whose mercy
    saved them all.

A deed like this could not be hid.   Upon the wings
    of fame,
To ev'ry corner of our isle, flew forth Grace Dar-
    ling's name ;
And tongues were loud in just applause, and bo-
    soms highly beat,

And tributes from the great and good were lavished
    at her feet;
While she, who braved the midnight blast, and rode
    the stormy swell,
Shrank timid, trembling, from the praise that she
    had earned so well.

Why did they tempt her forth to scenes she ill was
    formed to share ?
Why bid her face the curious crowd, the question,
    and the stare ?
She did not risk her life that night to earn the
    world's applause:
Her own heart's impulse sent her forth in pity's
    holy cause.
And richly were her toils repaid, and well her soul
    content
With the sweet thought of duty done, of succour
    timely lent.

Her tender spirit sinks apace.   O, bear the droop-
　　ing flower
Back to its native soil again—its own secluded
　　bower !
Amidst admiring multitudes, she sighs for home
　　and rest :
Let the meek turtle fold her wing within her own
　　wild nest ;
And drink the sights and sounds she loves, and
　　breathe her wonted air,
And find with them a quiet hour for thoughtful-
　　ness and prayer !

And she has reach'd her sea-girt home—and she can
　　smile once more ;
But ah, a faint and moonlight smile, without the
　　glow of yore !
The breeze breathes not as once it did upon her
　　fever'd brow ;

The waves talk on, but in her breast awake no
    echoes now :
For vague and flickering are her thoughts, her soul
    is on the wing
For Heaven, and has but little heed for earth or
    earthly thing.

"My Father, dost thou hear their shriek ? dost hear
    their drowning cry ?"
" No, dearest, no ; 'twas but the scream of the cur-
    lew flitting by."
Poor panting, fluttering, hectic thing, thy tossings
    soon will cease,
Thou art passing through a troubled sea, but to a
    land of peace !
And He, who to a shipwreck'd world brought rescue,
    O may He
Be near thy dying pillow now, sweet Grace, to
    succour thee !

LONGINGS FOR HOME.

STERN Britain, why a home deny
To one who loves thee well as I?
Who woos thee with as warm a zeal
As sons for tenderest mothers feel,
Would hold to thee through good and ill,
Yet finds thee but a Step-dame still?
Earth has for me no place of rest
So dear as thy parental breast,
No spot to which so close I cling
As to the shelter of thy wing;
And yet thou spurn'st me from thee, yea,
Spurn'st like a prodigal away;

Thou fling'st me suppliant from thy side,
To float a wreck upon the tide;
A boundless world at will to roam,
And sigh and think of thee and home!

Here, amidst fabled woods and streams,
The classic haunts of youthful dreams,
'Mid crumbling fanes and ruins hoary,
Rich with the hues of antique glory;
Where every hill and every dell
Has its own stirring tale to tell,
And thoughtful pilgrims oft compare
The things that are with things that were.
Yes, here, where seems so much combined
To soothe the sense and fill the mind,
All rich, all bright, around, above,
And soft as is the voice of love,—
While at my feet in silver flakes
The evening billow gently breaks,—

I stand and muse, and o'er the sea,
My thoughts roam off to home and thee.

O what is all that earth bestows,
All that mere sense enjoys and knows,
The fairest fields, the sunniest skies,
To life's diviner charities ?
Perchance this eve, so lovely here,
In my own land is bleak and drear;
And clouded skies and blustry weather,
Drive my own dear Ones close together;
And round the hearth their beaming faces
Perhaps take now their wonted places,
Each with his little social mite
To aid the general stock to-night;—
His flowret on Time's path to fling,
Or add a feather to his wing.
O, loved Ones, at this happy season
Of tender thought and social reason,

When hearts are full, and fancy free,
O do you sometimes think of me ?—
Think of your absent wanderer, who
So fondly hangs on home and you,
And would this moment rather share
Your homely fireside converse there,
And smile with you 'neath wintry skies,
Than reign in this fair paradise ?

Alas ! 'tis by their loss alone
Our truest blessings oft are known.
If earth wears here a sunnier hue,
Man is the plant that thrives with you ;
A plant matured by want and toil,
And noblest oft on poorest soil.
If bleak your hills and rough your clime,
They are not rank with weeds of crime ;
The social virtues there take root,
And freedom bears her richest fruit,

While industry and skill supplies
What niggard nature else denies.
The poor man's rights have honour due,
The wronged and weak redress with you.
And boundless as yon subject sea,
Large as the world, your charity.
Within your happy homes meanwhile
Order, and peace, and comfort smile;
And fertile are your rugged lands
In manly minds, and hearts, and hands,
In generous aims and thoughts elate,
And all that makes men good and great.
And more than all to you is given
High intercourse with God and heaven.
Religion walking through your land
Showers down her gifts with liberal hand,
And bids the desert, as she goes,
Rejoice and blossom like the rose.
This is thy glory, Britain; this

Makes thy fair Island what it is—
With all its faults, in moral worth,
The Eden of this fallen earth.

O gifts too lightly valued—how
My thirsty soul would prize them now!
Those hallowed Sabbaths, calm and fair,
That still well-ordered house of prayer,
The call that bids the weary come,
The ray that lights the wanderer home;
The Spirits whisper from above
The still small voice of truth and love.
O when, my own loved lost Ones, when
Shall we such blessings share again?
Drink of the sacred springs that flow
With balm for every want and woe,
Lift up our hearts in prayer and praise
Bequeathed from wiser, better days,

E

And round the Holy altar fare
On food that Angels may not share ?—
When shall such joys be ours ?   From high
Heard I a solemn voice reply :
" Live to your Saviour : watch and pray.
Grow in His image day by day ;
And know the Souls which thus improve
In meekness, duty, faith, and love,
Though severed in this world of pain,
In earth or Heaven shall meet again !"

Naples, Christmas, 1844.

THOUGHTS IN WEAKNESS.

PART I.

ENCOURAGEMENT.

THREE mighty companies compose
   The armies of the Lord ;
Upon His love they all repose,
   And wait upon His word.
Unlike the offices they fill,
   The homage that they bring,
But one their ceaseless object still
   To glorify their King.

The first in rank and station—they
   The bright angelic train,

Who never bowed 'neath sorrow's sway,
  Nor felt corruption's stain.
And yet they feel for man's distress,
  His every trial share,
Nor spurn the meanest services
  To help salvation's heir.

The next—a band of humbler birth,—
  But scarce of humbler place,
Who fought and bled for Christ on earth,
  And triumphed through His grace.
Their secret wrestlings, hidden life,
  To Him were not unknown :
His arm sustained them through the strife,
  And now they share His throne.

The last are they who still maintain
  The conflict here below,

Whose portion still is sin and pain,
　The danger and the foe.
They oft are foil'd, they oft despair,
　But help from high is given ;
They struggle on through faith and prayer,
　And fight their way to heaven.

And these—though poor and weak they be,
　The Saviour owns them still ;
They serve Him, though imperfectly,
　And yearn to work His will.
Temptation's tide they strive to stem,
　Though faith at times burns dim,
Nor find the Lord deserting them,
　While they depend on Him.

The world, the flesh, the Evil One,
　Assault them hour by hour ;
And soon must all their hopes be gone,
　If left to Nature's power.

But arm'd by Christ's own plighted word,
 When fiercest foes assail,
They meet them with the Spirit's sword,
 Nor find the weapon fail.

O mighty is the power of prayer,
 The promise large and true ;
The feeblest heart need not despair
 With these to bear it through.
Though darkest clouds o'ercast the sky,
 Though wave call out to wave,
Enough to know the Saviour nigh,
 To bless, to guide, to save.

Shall flesh and blood presume to shrink
 While He vouchsafes to aid ?
Shall nature hear that voice and sink,—
 " 'Tis I, be not afraid ?"
Behold—'tis Jesus walks the deck ;
 What fears our hearts o'erwhelm ?

Can wildest waves the vessel wreck
　While He is at the helm?

O, strange our courage e'er should reel
　With Him so near and kind;
So often rescued,—yet to feel
　So trustless and so blind!
O, strange to know all Heaven to be
　Upon our side arrayed,
All cheering, strengthening us, and we
　By every breath dismayed!

Go ask those victors now on high
　What help'd them on to Heaven,—
The very arms, they all reply,
　To you as freely given.
Our hearts, like your's, were faint and frail,
　Our foes as hard to tame;
But grace we found o'er all prevail.
　Oh, try and find the same!

PART II.

SUBMISSION.

Yet think not, O, my Soul, to keep
　　Thy progress on to God,
By any road less rough and steep
　　Than that thy Fathers trod.
In tears and trials thou must sow
　　To reap in joy and love.
We cannot find our home below,
　　And hope for one above.

No—here we labour, watch, and pray,
　　Our rest and peace are there—
God will not take the thorn away,
　　But gives us strength to bear.
The holiest, greatest, best have thus
　　In wisdom learnt to grow:

Yea, He that gave Himself for us
   Was perfected by woe.

Thou—Man of Sorrows,—Thou didst not
   The bitter cup decline.
Why should I claim a better lot,
   A smoother path than Thine ?
Thou sought'st no treasure here on earth,
   No glory 'neath the skies ;
And what Thou deem'dst so little worth,
   Shall I so highly prize ?

Did not reproach and wrong rain down
   Upon Thy hallowed head ?
Didst Thou not strip off glory's crown
   To wear the thorns instead ?
When foes reviled didst Thou reply,
   Or render ill for ill ?
Didst Thou for man bleed, faint, and die ;
   And shall I falter still ?

In early life to Thee I was
    Consigned by solemn vow :
Enlisted 'neath Thy Holy Cross,
    Shall I desert it now ?
I then, 'gainst ev'ry hostile power,
    Engaged to follow Thee ;
And shall I, at the trying hour,
    Be found the first to flee ?

Thou didst not flee, O King of Love,
    When Thou wert sorely tried ;
When all men fled, and God above
    Appeared His face to hide.
Intent That guiltless Blood to shed
    That should for guilt atone,
The mighty wine-press Thou did'st tread,
    Unshrinking, though alone.

And shall I murmur or repine
    At aught Thy Hand may send ?

To whom should I my cause resign,
   If not to such a Friend?
Where Love and Wisdom deign to choose,
   Shall I the choice condemn;
Or dare the medicine to refuse
   That is prescribed by them?

Oh, small the gain when men aspire
   Their Maker to control.
He gives, perhaps, their hearts' desire,
   And leanness to their soul.
Not His to quench the smoking flax,
   Or break the bruised reed;
Or with one pang our patience tax,
   But what He knows we need.

Yet must our stedfastness be tried,—
   Yet must our graces grow
By holy warfare. What beside
   Did we expect below?

Is not the way to Heavenly gain
    Through earthly grief and loss ?
Rest must be won by toil and pain—
    The Crown repays the Cross.

As woods, when shaken by the breeze,
    Take deeper, firmer root,
As winter's frosts but make the trees
    Abound in summer fruit;
So every Heaven-sent pang and throe
    That Christian firmness tries,
But nerves us for our work below,
    And forms us for the skies.

PART III.

ACTION.

Away then causeless doubts and fears
  That weaken and enthral;
Wipe off, my Soul, thy faithless tears,
  And rise to duty's call.
How much is there to win and do,
  How much to help and cheer!
The fields are white, the labourers few;
  Wilt thou sit 'plaining here?

Awake, my Soul, to duty wake;
  Go pay the debt thou ow'st.
Go forward,—and the night shall break
  Around thee as thou go'st.
A Red Sea may before thee flow,
  Egyptian hosts pursue;

But He that bids thee onward go
　　Will ope a pathway too.

Swift fly the hours, and brief the time
　　For action or repose ;—
Fast flits this scene of woe and crime,
　　And soon the whole shall close ;
The evening shadows deeper fall,
　　The daylight dies away.
Wake, slumberer, at the Master's call,
　　And work while it is day!

Rome, April 17, 1845.

THE CZAR IN ROME.

THE mighty Cæsar of the North
   Has entered Rome to-day.
Why peal her bells no greetings forth,
   Her crowds no tributes pay ?
"Stranger, we love the great and good;
But honour not the Man of blood [1]!

"The Man of blood! Can one so high
   Upon the lists of fame,

[1] In December, 1845, the Emperor Nicholas of Russia, after being at Palermo and Naples, came to Rome, but met with no welcome or greeting there. His reputation had come before him, and all were indignant at his tyrannical conduct towards his Polish subjects, and his persecution of the unfortunate Roman Catholics in his dominions, whom he wished to compel to conform to the Greek Church.

Who looks and moves thus royally,
    Deserve so dark a name ?"
" Yes ! let the pining Exile tell,
    The bleeding Martyr say, how well!"

While through these streets he sweeps to-day,
    The gaze of thousand eyes,
A victim of his iron sway
    In yonder convent lies [1],
And pleads for her oppressor there.—
O King of kings, fulfil her prayer!

The soul that looks through such an eye,
    That sits on such a brow;

[1] One of the unfortunate nuns from the convent of Minsk, of whom more than thirty had perished under the frightful persecutions to which they were subjected, escaped from Russia, and found her way to Rome, and was thus in a great measure the means of informing the world of the cruelties that were going on in Russia.

Must have its instincts rare and high,
　　Though undeveloped now ;
And moral music, strong and deep,
Among its chords must surely sleep [1].

And who shall say, within that breast
　　What throes e'en now may work ?
Seems there no sign of strange unrest
　　Beneath that brow to lurk ?
No troubled wave to heave and roll
O'er the proud stillness of his soul ?

This morn St. Peter's courts he trod,
　　With stately step and stern,
Encounter'd there the man of God ;—
　　And how did he return ?

[1] The Emperor Nicholas is said to be the finest looking man in Europe.

F

With faltering foot, and darken'd look,
That spoke confusion and rebuke[1].

Did some strong truth, all new and strange,
   Blest by the great " I am,"
Drop from those reverend lips, and change
   The Lion to the Lamb ?
Did pride feel there abash'd and awed,
And conscience own the voice of God ?

This morn before St. Peter's shrine
   In lowly guise he knelt.
Fell on him there some Grace divine,
   With power to move and melt ?

[1] The Emperor, the morning after his arrival, had an audience with the Pope, who appears to have spoken with great firmness and dignity upon the occasion ; and when the Emperor left his presence his face was flushed, the sweat stood on his brow, and he was evidently ill at ease.

And flew to him some wing of Love
Charged with an unction from above[1]?

While prostrate 'neath that ample dome,
    Amidst the holy dead,
Touch'd with the claims of injured Rome,
    His soul may well have said,
" Surely the Lord is in this spot,
And I, insensate, knew it not!"

Might one such feeling reach his heart,
    One thought like this prevail,
" Remember, mortal, what thou art,
    Accountable and frail!"

[1] After leaving the Pope, the Emperor went into St. Peter's, where he seemed awed with the majesty of the place, and fell prostrate before St. Peter's shrine, and kissed the ground. (The Greeks are worshippers of the saints, even more than the Roman Catholics.) It is even said, that there he told his attendants, that if the Roman Catholics had been persecuted in Russia, they should be so no more.

The crowns and sceptres of this earth,
Weigh'd with that thought, had little worth.

And where so well might moods like these
   Upon the spirit come
As here, where sighs the autumn breeze
   O'er desolated Rome;
Where every stone its moral brings;
Where tread we on the dust of kings?

Saw ye a shadowy hand sublime
   Write on that ruin'd wall?
Heard ye a voice, the voice of Time,
   From yon grey turret call?
" All fleets, all fades beneath the skies;
O man, be humble and be wise!"

Go forth then, King of nations: march
   Along the Sacred way;

Stand 'neath the yet unbroken arch
　　Of him who lost a day,
When he had done no generous deed;
And wilt thou there no lesson read [1] ?

Go where the Coliseum rears
　　Its sad, majestic pile,—
The pride and shame of former years :—
　　Go, when the moonbeams smile,
And talk with the historic dead,
Who there have revell'd,—or have bled !

The Tyrant's trophies sink to dust [2] ;
　　The Hero's still arise,

[1] A friend of mine saw the Emperor twice standing in meditative mood under the arch of Titus; and he paid three visits to the Coliseum.

[2] It is remarked, that the only monumental remains now standing at Rome are, with one trifling exception, such as were erected to commemorate the lives and actions of the most vir-

True to their monumental trust,—
    Lo, in the evening skies,
How freshly bright the columns shine
    Of Trajan and of Antonine!

Go, then, to these mute teachers; go!
    And if, like genial rain,
Their lore upon thy heart shall flow,
    Thou cam'st not here in vain;
Nor shalt thou fail to carry home
A blessing from Eternal Rome!

tuous of her ancient heroes. The most perfect of these remains
are the pillars of Trajan and Antoninus, the most excellent of
her rulers.

FRAGMENTS

OF AN UNFINISHED POEM, ENTITLED LILLA.

A FAIRY TALE.

*　　*　　*　　*　　*　　*

'Tis pleasant to walk the broad sea-shore
When the soul is dark, or the heart is sore.
The waves give forth a soothing sound,
As they boom along the shelving ground;
The crispness of the salt-sea air
Breathes fresh on the fever'd brow of care:
And the waters, melting into the sky,
Send the spirit on to Eternity!
So felt Sir Rupert, as o'er the sands
That skirted his own brave house and lands

He paced, but in dark regardless mood
Of aught that there his attention woo'd.

The sky was clear, and the sun was bright,
The blue waves danced in the shifting light,
And the foam-bells on the sand uproll'd
Like silvery fret on a floor of gold.
The far white ships sail'd stately by,
The seamew flitted and laugh'd on high.
But all appear'd in vain to woo
Sir Rupert's thoughts to a livelier hue.

*   *   *   *   *   *

From that mysterious race I'm sprung
That lived with man, when the world was young:
But ever since envy and lust possess'd,
And ruled and sullied his own pure breast,
They have fled from earthly folly and art,
And dwell in a world of their own apart:
Hiding in Nature's secluded bowers,
Watching and tending her fruits and flowers,

Giving the blossom its scent and hue,
And the fainting leaf its drink of dew ;
Spanning the shower with its bright brief arch
Leading the seasons their stately march,
Staying the storm in his fierce career.—
These are the tasks which engage us here.
Not that we less count man our friend,
Or fail on his homely wants to tend.
We note the housewife's honest cares,
And speed her labours all unawares.
We succour the mower down in the mead,
And help the ploughman to sow his seed.
We smoothe the pillow where sickness lies,
And shake sweet sleep o'er the infant's eyes.
But we mingle not in man's vain affairs,
Nor darken our path with his fears and cares ;
And the Court, the City, the festive hall,
We feel as strangers amidst them all.

*   *   *   *   *   *

'Tis merry, 'tis merry in Colmar towers,
On Rostan's hills, and in Binda's bowers,
In humble cot, and in stately hall;
There are happy looks and hearts in all.
The cloud that hung o'er the whole is fled,
And the broad clear sun laughs out instead.
One influence sweet, one presence bright,
Has quicken'd the darkness into light.
Woman's soft smile is in Colmar found,
And it blesses and gladdens all around.
This Rupert felt, as from day to day
Lilla spread round her gentle sway;
All, all beneath her influence grew
To a better tone, to a brighter hue.
Old Colmar's courts no longer wore
Their lorn and desolate air of yore;
A cheerful bustle ran through the place,
Content sat beaming on every face;
And active feet and diligent hands,

Eager to work her light commands;
And all on their various tasks intent,
At their Lady's bidding came and went.
All into life by her eye seem'd warm'd;
All to her own sweet will conform'd;
Till throughout that grim old gothic pile
Order and neatness began to smile;
And comfort lighted up there a home
That stole from the heart all wish to roam.

Nor less did improvement win its way
O'er all that around the castle lay.
The lawn, of late so rugged and wild,
Like emerald velvet now glow'd and smiled.
The walk with mosses and weeds o'erspread
Woo'd the light step o'er its gravelly bed.
Trees and shrubs that had wont to swing
Their long lank arms on the wild-wind's wing,
Were taught to conform their savage will
To the eye of taste and the hand of skill.

The fount, that long had forgot to play,
Sparkled once more in the morning ray.
The vine clung again to the elm-tree tall,
And the plum hung blue on the garden wall.—
And then the flowers, the laughing flowers,
The playmates of Lilla's earliest hours,
How did she revel among them! how
Watch, and nurse, and enjoy them now!
Whether they grew on the wild bank, known
To the wandering bee and the lark alone;
Or bloom'd in the garden's courtly bed,
Like orient beauties in harem bred;
From the queen-like rose to the harebell small,
Gentle and simple she loved them all.

She loved whatever was lovely here;
And flowers, sweet flowers, to her heart were dear.
She knew their ways, and her joy and pride
Was to gather them round her from every side,

To give them the site which themselves would choose,
To trim their leaves, and to match their hues;
A staff in the weak one's hand to place,
And lift to the sun its small pale face;
To bring the diffident out to view,
The bold to check, and the proud subdue.
Not one of them all but had its share
Of her watchful love and judicious care.
She flitted among them as if on wings,
And talk'd to them all as to living things.
And they as conscious how great their bliss,
Held up their cheeks for a passing kiss;
Flung in her pathway their sweetest scent,
And smiled and nodded as on she went.

*   *   *   *   *   *

They wander down to the broad sea-shore,
But not in his once dark spirit of yore.
Now, not a wild wing that across them flies,
Not a light shell in their path that lies,

Nothing in ocean, or earth, or sky,
Fails to awaken their sympathy.
Or, if the sun with his fiercer rays
Drives their steps to the woodland ways,
The squirrel is there with his chattering glee,
And the jay glad shouting from tree to tree;
And the rabbit stirring the ferns among,
And the pheasant sunning her speckled young,
O! nature a golden harvest yields
To all who will glean in her varied fields;
But their brightest tints her objects wear
When those that we love are nigh to share!

* * * * * *

And O! she was rich in each social wile,
The night of its weariness to beguile!
She spoke, and mute attention hung,
Persuasion dwelt on her silver tongue;
Sweet fancies, clad in sweetest words,
Held the charm'd ear with magic cords,

And judgment clear, and taste refined,
Brought food alike to the heart and mind.
And when her favourite songs she sung,
The birds stay'd theirs ;—the soft winds hung
Entranced around her to catch the tone,
And by her music to mend their own.

*   *   *   *   *   *

Each lived for each, one will, one heart;
Without a thought or a wish apart.
As streams, from opposite hills that run,
But meet in the valley, and blend in one,
Their murmurs hush'd, and their wanderings past,
Glide on together in peace at last !

*   .*   *   *   *   *

SONG.

Weep on ! weep on ! 'tis a world of woe ;
'Tis vain to expect aught else below.
The life of man has but one true tone,
From its infantile cry, to its dying groan.

Each step he takes through a land of gloom,
But carries him onward to the tomb;
And all that he meets with as he goes
Talks to his heart of the solemn close.

Weep on! there are many with man to
  weep,
The murmuring winds, and the moaning deep;
The fading flower, and the falling dews,
And the year expiring in dolphin hues.
What says the rainbow's beautiful dream?
Or the sunset's brief but gorgeous gleam?
Or the summer lightning, now come, now gone?—
We shine but to fade! Weep on! weep on!

Weep on! it is good on this earth to weep:
If we sow in tears, we in joy may reap.
While the hopes that we madly cherish there
But pave the way to some new despair.

Pale is the young cheek's richest bloom
When it strews the path to an early tomb;
And dim the fire of the brightest eye
When a beacon that points to mortality.

Weep on! weep on!   *   *   *

THE

COMPLAINT OF MARY MAGDALENE.

She sat far off,—she sat and wept,
  Heart-broken Magdalene!
Her dark and silent watch she kept
  Throughout the awful scene.
No power had she to soothe or aid,
  No hope to interpose;
Yet love and grief her heart upstaid
  To watch Him to the close.

'Twas He, 'twas He, who first the way
  Of life to her had shown;
Had freed her soul from Satan's sway,
  And made it all His own.

'Twas He she soon had hoped to see
 In Kingly glory rise,—
And now, upon the fatal Tree,
 He bleeds, He faints, He dies!

And she has follow'd Him through all
 His wrongs and griefs to-day,
Stood with Him in the Judgment Hall,
 Trod o'er the public way.
The scourge, the cords, the savage thorns,
 She shared them to the close;
Scorn'd in her outraged Master's scorns,
 And bleeding in His woes.

The ponderous Cross she saw Him bear,
 All fainting up the Hill;
She saw them nail Him on it there
 With unrelenting skill;

She heard their wild and withering cry
  As He aloft was swung,
The gaze of every flashing eye,
  The scoff of every tongue !

No angel comes, on wings of love,
  His sinking soul to cheer;
The very Heavens seem shut above,
  And Mercy fails to hear;
Despised, deserted, crush'd, and awed,
  He hangs upon the tree,
And cries in vain, " My God, My God,
  Hast Thou forsaken me ?"

O trying scene for woman's eye !
  And yet she braved it all;
The struggle and the agony,
  The wormwood and the gall,—

Though earth beneath in horror shook,
   Though Heaven its light withdrew,
And sterner hearts the awe partook,
   Yet woman braved it through.

She sat far off—she sat and wept,
   Heart-broken Magdalene !
Her dark and silent watch she kept
   Throughout the trying scene !
She sank not when His head He bow'd,
   She bore His dying groan—
Till pass'd away the sated crowd,
   And left her there alone !

The shades of evening round her head
   Now gather'd thick and fast ;
And forth her burthen'd spirit fled
   In louder woe at last.

Upon the ear of silent night,
  Her plaintive murmurs broke,
And sorrow seem'd to grow more light
  As thus she wept and spoke.—

" And is all over ?   Can it be
  That they have had their will ?
Thou hanging, Lord, on yonder tree,
  And we surviving still ?
Is this to be the course and close
  Of all Thy conflicts past ?
A brief, dark path through wrongs and woes
  To such a death at last ?

" Yes, past all reach of ill Thou art,—
  I see no living sign ;
And, O, that this sad struggling heart
  Were now as still as Thine !

I groan—Thou canst not heed my groan,
   Nor answer when I plain.—
Ah! I shall never hear the tone
   Of that blest voice again.

" O hallow'd head! compell'd to bow
   Beneath unnumber'd scorns;
O dear, dishonour'd, glorious brow,
   Now crush'd beneath the thorns;
O eyes, where Heaven-seem'd once to reign,
   Can ye grow glazed and dim?
O death, by Him for others slain,
   Canst thou have power o'er Him?

" How could'st thou, brutal soldier, dare
   To pierce that breast divine?—
There never dwelt a feeling there
   But love to thee and thine.

How could ye harm one tender limb
   Of His, ye murderous crew,
And know that while ye tortured Him
   He pray'd for you, for you?

" It must be right, I feel it must,
   Though all is darkness now ;—
Lord, teach my trembling heart to trust,
   And help my will to bow !
'Tis hard upon that Cross to gaze,
   Nor feel the Tempter's power.
O God ! sustain me through the maze
   Of this mysterious hour !

" Yes ! mystery o'er the whole doth hang,
   To be unravelled still.
Who could on Him inflict a pang
   Without the Sufferer's will ?

He, whom the slumbering dead have heard,
  Whose voice the winds could tame,
Could not He crush them with a word
  If such had been His aim ?

" But I remember well, when hope
  Seem'd most our hearts to cheer,
What hints and warnings He would drop
  Of pain and trial near.
He, doubtless, was intent to give
  A lesson here from high ;
And as He taught us how to live,
  Would teach us now to die !

" Yet surely 'twas a loftier task
  That drew Him from the skies,
And ne'er could mere example ask
  So dire a sacrifice ;—

And surely these were all to tend
  At last to brighter bliss,
Not prematurely here to end
  In double night like this.

"All prophecy proclaims a time
  When Satan's rule shall cease,
When Earth shall pass from woe and crime
  To endless love and peace,—
When Death and Hell with all their hosts
  Shall quail before their Lord,
And more than was in Adam lost
  Shall be in Christ restored.

"Yes, Lord of lords, and King of kings,
  For such Thou art to me,
My soul through doubt and darkness clings
  With trembling faith to Thee,—

I feel some brighter morn will yet,
  Our shatter'd hopes surprise,
And glory's sun, that now is set,
  Again in glory rise.

" The great Messiah still Thou art,
  Confirm'd by every sign;
And this may all be but a part
  Of some sublime design.
What God ordains must needs be best,—
  What He permits is right;
On Him, on Him my soul I rest,
  And wait for further light.

" One mournful task is left me too,
  Thy dear remains to tend;
With honours due Thy bier to strew,
  And watch Thee to the end.

Then let me to Thy lifeless clay
  Still sadly, fondly cling,
And wait, and weep, and hope, and pray
  For what the day may bring."—

She said, and seem'd to ease her breast
  In these complaints and prayers;
Then rose, and went to seek the rest,
  And mingle tears with theirs.
She went the spices to provide,
  His last sad rites to pay,—
Then by the tomb sat down and sigh'd,
  " O, when will it be day ?"

JANUARY 1st, 1847.

What solemn footfall smote my startled ear?
Heard I the step of the departing year?
Saw I her shadowy form flit slowly by,
To join her sisters in eternity?—
Sweeping down thither, as the autumn's blast
Sweeps summer's leaves, the records of the past,
The joys and griefs, the bustle and the strife,
The shadows and realities of life?
Hear me, stern daughter of old Time, O hear!—
Is there no plea may stay thy strong career?
O pause in pity! pause, and to my prayer
Grant a brief converse with the things that were—
I know the retrospect has much to pain,
Much to be mended could all come again;

Still, without one last look we must not sever,
Sad is the word that bids to part for ever!
Beam, then, again on me, dear, kindly faces,
And smile your best, old times and well-known
          places;
Bright looks, soft tones, high thoughts, and fancies
          fair,
Return, return, and be what once you were!
All that was precious in the year that's past,—
Too sweet to lose, too beautiful to last—
Sunshine, and song, and fragrance, things that
          threw
O'er life's dull path a brighter tint and hue;
Hopes realized, desires fulfill'd;—success
Crowning long toils; the burthens of distress
Lighten'd, Will subjugated, self-denied,
Ills overcome by long endurance, Pride
Taught to be greatly humble,—all that wakes
The approving voice of conscience, all that makes

Heaven's windows open o'er us, converse sweet,—
And sweeter meditation ; all,—all fleet
Back into being.—Burst oblivion's chain,
And be awhile realities again !—

Blest be the powers that can the past restore ;—
They come, they come, warm breathing as of
　　　　　yore !
I hear remember'd voices, seem to dwell
Once more with forms I've known and loved so
　　　　　well.
Distinct, beyond my fondest hopes, they rise,
The shadows dimming the realities.
Beautiful witcheries !　O would I might
Hold them thus ever, durable as bright !
But, like the splendours of a sunset sky,
E'en while I gaze their glories wane and die,
And, as they fade, uprising in their rear
A host of darker verities appear ;

Sorrows and sins of various shade and hue,
That claim their notice in the year's review.
And shall they be rejected ? shall my eyes
Be shut to life's too stern realities ?
And shall the records of the past be seen,
Not as they were, but as they should have been ?
No ! small the gain and brief the joy that lives
In the poor dreams such self-delusion gives ;
And honest conscience scorns to take a tone,
Or speak a flattering language not her own ;
And wherefore seek to bribe her, wherefore fear
Her rough but salutary voice to hear,
When every warning, now rejected, grows
To overwhelming thunder at the close?

The close ! the close ! How like a death-knell seems
That solemn word to wake me from my dreams !
One little year, yea, less than one like this,
May bring me to the close of all that is.

Far down Time's chequered stream I've voyaged
    on,
And seen my fellows drop off, one by one ;
And now the widening waters seem to near
Eternity's dark ocean ; on my ear
Sound the deep heavings of that shoreless sea,
And awe my soul into solemnity !
Darkling I hover round the world to come,
And voices thence are heard to call me home ;
And stretching on into the dread expanse,
I fain would lift the curtain, and advance.
One little step, I know, would bear me through,
And give the secrets of the dead to view ;
But till that step is taken, mortal sense,
Ask as it may, gets no response from thence.
Thought may at times, when all around me sleep,
Launch sounding forth into that silent deep ;
But without star to guide or light to cheer,
Soon back to land my trembling course I steer.

II

Even bold Conjecture onward fears to fare,
And Reason shrinks to find no footing there;
Till conscious Nature, baffled and o'er-awed,
Sinks suppliant on the Mercy of her God,
Turns from self-confidence to faith and prayer,
Clings to His Word, and finds her refuge there.

Thrice happy we, not left to grope our way
From truth to truth, by Nature's feeble ray,
Where one false step were ruin.   Happier still
Our wills conforming to the Heavenly Will;
Ready, as God may prompt, to think, and feel,
And take His impress, as the wax the seal;
At His blest feet content to sit and learn,
Or walk by faith, till faith to sight shall turn;
Beneath the Saviour's cross to stand and scan
All He has done, and all He claims from man;
Learn from His life, and on His death repose,
And grow in love and duty to the close.

On the year's threshold, on the narrow strand
That parts the past and future, here I stand,
Without control o'er either: one is flown
Beyond recal;—a dark and dread unknown,
The other stretches onward,—what to be,
Seen but by Him who fills Eternity.
The present, and scarce that, is still my own;—
Oh, be it consecrate to Heaven alone!
Be mine, while all things shift and change around,
To cleave to Him in whom no change is found,
To rest on the Immutable, to cling
Closer and closer 'neath the Almighty wing;
His voice in all its varied tones to hear,
And in all aspects feel Him ever near;
Be mine with Him to walk, on Him depend,
Then, come what may, it all to good must tend!

Rome.

THE POET'S PLEA.

DEAL gently with the poet. Think that he
  Is made of finer clay than other men,
And ill can bear rough handling; and while we,
  Of sturdier natures, laugh'd at laugh again,
And self-complacently shake off
The world's unmerited contempt and scoff—
As easily as from his scaly side
Leviathan shakes off the drippings of the tide;—
Not so the poet. On his keener sense
Light harms smite often with an edge intense.
A stony look, a lip of scorn, may crush
His young aspirings; chill the stir and flush
Of waking inspiration; and control
Down into common-place the darings of his soul.

Lightly his spirit touch!
The lyre is delicate; the chords are fine;
And fine must be the finger, that from such
    Wins melody divine.
The strings, that gentler skill to music wakes,
    A clash impetuous breaks.
And images, that, in the musing mind,
As in a placid lake, lie mirrored and defined,
If ruffling winds along the surface stray,
Scatter'd and broken, pass like rack away.
Stored thoughts and treasured feelings, that in
      turn
Were ready to leap forth, and breathe, and burn
In verse, as fancy called them, once dispersed,
Bide, like the Sibyl's leaves, unscanned and unre-
      hearsed.

    And, Desolater, who shall say
Of what thy rashness may have 'reft mankind?

Take the sweet poetry of life away,
    And what remains behind ?
O, who his seventy years would delve and plod,
And tug through life's dull tide the weary oar,
Were all his heritage what earth's poor clod
    Can yield, and nothing more ?
Perhaps the Poet had that moment caught
Some hallowed truth, some spirit-stirring thought,
That—like the wakening of a trumpet blast,—
From age to age might thrillingly have pass'd.
Perhaps some happy fancy, some fair dawn
Of beauty, on his mind may just have shone;—
Some touch of holy tenderness, whose spell
Might melt and mend all hearts whereon it
    fell.
He was, perhaps, aloft among the stars,—
Perhaps beyond them; leaning on the bars,
    The golden bars, that Heaven enclose,
    List'ning the music that within—

A vocal glory, fell and rose
From lips of chaunting seraphin;
Intent to carry down from thence
All that could enter mortal sense,
Dull'd as it is by sin;—
And thou did'st call him down from tasks like these,
To mix with common life's poor, tame formalities!

Go, Man of earth, and do thy work! obey
Thy five good senses! Traffic, drudge, design!
To small civilities due homage pay!—
The Poet has his province, and thou thine.
He dwells within a sphere thou can'st not enter,
Nearer the throne, fast by the mighty centre;
And hears what cannot reach the unchasten'd ear
Of those who stand outside, among the million
here.
To thee and thine belong the Gentile courts,
To which the uncircumcised crowd resorts.

He finds admittance to the inmost shrine,
Which none can hope to reach till led by hands
    divine.
Keep then thy place. Thou hast good work to
    do;
Not they alone the temple service share
Who tend the altar.   Those are needful too,
Who hew the wood and draw the water there.
The daily drudgery of life demands
A due relay of honest heads and hands;
They have their use; shall have their pay besides.
The world is just, and for her own provides.
To thrive in pelf, in pomp and place to shine;
These are her gifts, and these shall, Man of earth,
    be thine.
But trench not on the Poet's charter'd rights,
He walks his own domain with haughty brow:
His heavenly communings, his eagle flights
    Are not for such as thou.

High thoughts, warm feelings, the perennial spring
Of inward gladness, rapture's thrill and glow,
The heart in flower, the fancy on the wing,—
    Thou must not hope to know.
These are the Poet's dower.   Of these possest,
He smiles, and bids earth's minion take the rest!

But spare, ye men of fact, ye sapient band,
With critic lore, our desperate ears to stun.
Carp not at that you do not understand;
Nor spend your shafts in shooting at the sun.
The rich creations, which the Poet flings
In rainbow radiance from his passing wings,
You may not duly relish, rightly scan;
Yet think, wise sirs, there may be those who can;
And kill not his fine frenzies with your frown,
Nor to your standard seek to dwarf him down.
You prize the useful.   Be it so.   Yet tell,
In what consists this useful?   The Allwise,

In furnishing the world in which we dwell,
Stints not His gifts to mere necessities ;
Nor deems it waste to tint the bird's bright wing,
　　Yea, give him voice to sing ;
To beautify the flower, and to its bloom
　　To superadd perfume.
Things need not be fantastic nor unreal
　　Because they are ideal.
Nay, every object in this world of dreams
　　Is what to each it seems.
And that, which quickens into action all
Of good in man, that has survived the fall,
Refines each baser sense, and helps to call
From all that is, the good, the beautiful ;
That bids Experience half·her ills withhold,
And turns whate'er it touches into gold ;—
Can that be useless ? that, whose hallowing leaven
Imparts to this poor world whate'er it has of
　　Heaven ?

O empty Cavillers! why not assign
New laws to Nature, teach the stars to shine?
Soar through the clouds, proud gazer at the sun,
And leave the owls and bats at noonday to doze on!

Yet not the worldly, nor the dull alone
Refuse Heaven's favoured one his homage due:
Minds of a larger grasp and loftier tone
    Oft wrong the Poet too.
    O the half-hearted praise,
The chilling toleration, men can give
To powers, that mortals from the dust can raise
    Among the gods to live!
    Who shall the boons declare
With which the Poet sows our fallen earth?
The holy thoughts, and sweet emotions there,
    That owe to him their birth?
    High sentiments, now grown
Familiar household terms mankind among,

Are oft but sparklets of the soul, once thrown
From some poetic tongue;
Rich emanations of some pregnant mind,
Bright gems of thought in happy words enshrined;
That lend to common life a higher tone,
And touch within men's hearts, chords to them-
selves unknown.
And shall the Poet, like a kindled torch,
For us and ours in self-devotion burn,
And taunts that blister, and rebukes that scorch
Be dealt him in return?
Shall all his thoughtful toil,
His midnight watchings, solitude, and pain,
Ask the cheap meed of one approving smile,
And ask in vain?
Shall we prefer to sit
In cold, stern dignity, in Censure's chair,
When we with him on social wing might flit
Through ocean, earth, and air?

When we might rise and reign
In each high privilege to genius given,
Bright, living links of the electric chain
    Connecting earth with Heaven ?
O senseless choice! that frowns and stands apart,
When both might sweetly mingle, heart with heart!
O poor exchange, the critic's carps and sneers,
For poetry's full soul, her raptures, and her tears!

Make large allowance, then, for Nature's child;
School him not tamely down to rule and line.
Let the fine Savage roam his native wild;
Nor fetter Fancy's chartered libertine.
The stale observances to dulness dear,—
O chide not, if beyond their pale he rove,
And rise from Lar and the Penates here,
    To walk the Heavens with Jove.
Be his to pierce the wild wood's tangled maze,
And find or force new by-paths of his own.

The fruits are gathered by the beaten ways;
   The flowers are trampled down.
   Be his aloft to soar
Within the winnow of Archangel's wing,
And hear beneath his feet the thunder's roar,
   And the grim whirlwinds sing.
   Within the hearts of men,
Be his each secret chamber to unbar,
And drag the struggling passions from their den,
   To yoke them to his car.
Free, let him range the globe from land to land,
And some new lore from every object win:
Or by the flood of ages thoughtful stand,
And hear earth's Empires one by one drop in.
Calm let him sit by nature's mighty wheel,
To watch her workings, and her ways reveal,
Or launch abroad her silent depths to sound,
And bring up wonders for the world around.
Grand his ambitions!   Be his scope as grand!

They only greatly do, who greatly dare;
Why snatch the club from Hercules's hand
  To place the distaff there?
No! let him dally with the lightnings; fling
Forth, if he will, upon the tempest's wing;
Ride the careering billow without rein,
And stroke with playful hand its foamy mane;
And scorning by the servile shore to creep,
Forth let him steer to seek new worlds across the
  deep.

Yet should the worst befal, should wrongs assail,
Should envy harass, or indifference chill,
Should evil days and evil tongues prevail,
Be strong, O genius! much is left thee still.—
The by-path through the meads is warm and sweet;
Soft evening breezes from the orchards play;
Crush'd herbs give out their odours 'neath thy feet,
And flashing brooks dance by thee all the way.

The small shrill people of the grass
Chirp welcomes as they see thee pass ;—
The flowers unlock their hearts, and thence
Breathe odorous secrets forth to thy quick sense.

Dryads and fauns in woodland spaces,
Push through the leaves their laughing faces;
And bending boughs to thee make suit,
And to thy hand present their tributary fruit.

Thine are the living fountains,
That down the rocks in liquid silver run ;
Thine are the giant mountains,
That lift their broad green shoulders to the
sun.

The clouds that sail the summer sky,
Or o'er their shadows anchor high ;
The stars that round the matron moon
People with glory the blue vault of June,
All, all, are thine! From off her ample breast,
Sweet Nature, flinging wide her folded vest,

Gives thee her very self unveil'd to see,
And freely talks her inmost soul to thee.
Yea, and should these all fail thee, still thou hast
Thy solace; hast thy white, auspicious days,
When thoughts—like showering meteors, bright
       and fast,
Flash on thy soul, self-clad in aptest phrase.
Thou hast thy glorious visions of the night,
Mysterious converse with the mighty dead;—
Angelic visitants, from realms of light,
Ascending and descending o'er thy head.

    There may be toil.   While here,
Man in his sweat, his daily bread must eat;
Yet faint not.   There is much thy work to cheer,
The very pains of poetry are sweet.

    The streams which others' thirst supply
    Shall not be to their owner dry;
And precious draughts from thence shall bless,
And stay thy spirit through the wilderness.

A light shall guide thee better than the rules
The world employs to school her knaves and fools.
A happy instinct bears the Poet through;
And while he speaks and writes, he lives the Poet
      too.
And as·thou sitt'st and singest all apart,
Feeling it recompense enough to vent
The throbbing pulses of a pent-up heart,
And make the soul's mute yearnings eloquent;
     Those argosies of thought and rhyme
     Thou launchest on the stream of Time,
     Floating to unborn generations down,
Shall blessings bear to them, and to thyself renown.
     That which is truly noble cannot die!
     Eternal as its hallow'd course on high!
     Heroes and Conquerors have their day;
     Kings with their Empires pass away.
     Things, which to marble we entrust,
     Shall with it moulder into dust.

But one true flash of living mind,
At Heaven's own altar kindled and refined,
   Shall travel, like a beacon light,
   From intellectual height to height,
Unquenched, unquenchable! Seas cannot drown,
Mountains o'erwhelm it, legions tread it down;
A moment lost, 'tis sure again to rise,
And lead, from strength to strength, still onward
     to the skies.

Yet think, O mortal, think, while thus endow'd
With more than mortal privilege and power,
Think how they lift thee o'er the ignoble
     crowd,
Who walk by sense, and live but for the hour.
   Gifts that have had their birth
Beyond the everlasting hills on high,
Sent down to dwell awhile in hearts on earth,
Should still tend upward to their native sky.

Husks, that the swine do eat,
Earth's bursting bubbles, must not thee delight,
With Heaven's own Manna falling at thy feet,
And Canaan's promised glories full in sight.
　　No! be it thine to rise
In noble scorn of every meaner thing,
Self-buoyant, like the bird of paradise
That sleeps and wakes for ever on the wing.
The vestal fire must not be left to wane,
Nor lightly desecrate to use profane.
Thou walk'st this earth the delegate of Heaven;
And much shall be required where much is given.
Not that the tone need always be sublime;
The light and graceful have their place and time.
But for the loose, the impious, or the base,
Exists no privilege of time or place.
O, scorn them, scorn them! To thyself be
　　　　true!
Breathe not a thought thou e'er shalt wish unsaid;

Nought that may haunt and sadden life's review,
Or cast a shadow o'er thy dying bed.
Thine is a lofty mission. Nothing less
Than God to glorify, and Man to bless;
To raise poor grovelling Nature from the mire,
To give her wings, and teach her to aspire;
To nurse heroic moods; meek worth to cheer;
To dry on sorrow's cheek the trembling tear;
And still be ready, let who will deride,
To take the lists on injured Virtue's side.

    This is thy calling. Tasks like these
Claim and repay the soul's best energies.
Nor need'st thou fear, while thus employed,
That life should seem a burthen or a void.
Joys shall be thine, Man makes not, nor unmakes;—
Cheer, which the fickle world nor gives nor takes;—
Unhoped for streams that in the desert rise,
And sunshine bursting through the cloudiest skies!

From light to light thy steps shall tend,
Thy prospects ever brightening to the end;
Thy soul acquiring as it goes
The tone and feelings that befit the close.
Such path, O gifted one, be thine to tread!
And when the Judge of quick and dead
To each His sentence shall assign,
"Well done, thou faithful servant!" shall be thine!
And thou shalt rise the tasks of Heaven to share,
Join the blest choir, and feel no stranger there.
And "power and honour to the Lamb" shall seem
To thee no new and uncongenial theme.
The strains, to which thy earthly powers were given,
Shall be renew'd and perfected in Heaven;
And more than e'er blest Poet's dream, shall be
The Poet's portion there, throughout eternity!

Rome, March, 1847.

ABIDE WITH ME.

"Abide with us: for it is towards evening, and the day is far
spent." St. Luke xxiv. 29.

Abide with me! Fast falls the eventide;
The darkness deepens: Lord, with me abide!
When other helpers fail, and comforts flee,
Help of the helpless, O abide with me!

Swift to its close ebbs out life's little day;
Earth's joys grow dim; its glories pass away:
Change and decay in all around I see;
O Thou, who changest not, abide with me!

Not a brief glance I beg, a passing word,
But as Thou dwell'st with Thy disciples, Lord,

Familiar, condescending, patient, free,
Come, not to sojourn, but abide, with me!

Come not in terrors, as the King of kings;
But kind and good, with healing in Thy wings:
Tears for all woes, a heart for every plea.
Come, Friend of sinners, and thus bide with
      me!

Thou on my head in early youth didst smile,
And, though rebellious and perverse meanwhile,
Thou hast not left me, oft as I left Thee.
On to the close, O Lord, abide with me!

I need Thy presence every passing hour.
What but Thy grace can foil the Tempter's
      power?
Who like Thyself my guide and stay can be?
Through cloud and sunshine, O abide with me!

I fear no foe with Thee at hand to bless:
Ills have no weight, and tears no bitterness.
Where is death's sting? where, grave, thy victory?
I triumph still, if Thou abide with me.

Hold then Thy cross before my closing eyes;
Shine through the gloom, and point me to the skies:
Heaven's morning breaks, and earth's vain shadows
      flee.
In life and death, O Lord, abide with me!

Berryhead, September, 1847.

Early Poems.

THE

BATTLE OF SALAMANCA,

FOUGHT AGAINST THE FRENCH,

ON THE 22ND DAY OF JULY, 1812,

BY THE COMBINED ARMIES OF GREAT BRITAIN,

PORTUGAL, AND SPAIN,

UNDER THE COMMAND OF THE

MARQUIS OF WELLINGTON.

DEDICATION

TO THE MOST NOBLE

THE MARQUIS OF WELLESLEY.

An unfledged bard, who just had broke
From birch and grammar's awful yoke,
Would spread his glad unfetter'd wing,
And boldly try to croak or sing.
His bardic rites devoutly paid,
His Muses duly sought for aid,
When bitten nail and swollen cheek
A modern rapture seem'd to wake,
With scowling eye and muttering tongue,
For Fancy's topmost cloud he sprung,
As pride or madness led the way—
And here, behold, his first essay.

For, rushing on with epic aim,
He grasp'd Britannia's lists of fame,
To seek a Hero for the lays
Which, thus enrapt, he meant to raise:
A Hero round whose noble head
When Fancy's youthful hand had spread
A garland of the fairest flowers
·That ever bloom'd in Tempe's bowers,
Or hung their heads in airy pride
Around Castalia's *mirror* tide,
The voice of truth might still declare
Not half his honours gather'd there—
Though wide his search, he found but one,
One man like this—'twas Wellington!

For in his warm and generous mind
Such various virtues shone combined;
So great, yet simple seem'd he still,
So fired by valour, nerved by skill.

In others' cause so feeling known,
So lavish of himself alone,
That mortals seem'd on him to gaze
The phœnix of these later days,
Raised up the masterpiece of fate
For them to praise and imitate!
Like the bright arch that glows on high
When glooms and clouds invest the sky,
Mankind with veneration views
The lofty wonder's brightening hues,
And sees in his resplendent form
The queller of the blackening storm!

And could not reason, could not shame
Deter thee from that sacred theme?
But thou, poor witling, must profane
Such greatness with thy pigmy strain?
Perhaps thou deem'dst his name enough
To consecrate thy wretched stuff?

Or hopedst, at worst, with him to live,
Like Mævius pinn'd to Virgil's sleeve?

I own my folly, own my crimes;
I own them weak and wicked rhymes:
Yet, as the sire with partial care
Regards his crippled son and heir,
In spite of every shapeless feature,
I own, I own, I love the creature.
But bold by desperation grown,
I spurn at half a fault alone;
And bursting caution's barriers through,
For refuge would retreat to you,
Would join upon my humble page
The brother glories of the age,
Conscious that could my hopeless toil
From you obtain a favouring smile,
That Critic scarce would dare aspire
To blame what Wellesley should admire!

INTRODUCTION.

O'ER Europe's fields, all ravaged and forlorn,
   While Discord's dæmon leads his funeral train,
And every neighbouring state is doom'd to
         mourn,
   Or dread the horrors of a tyrant's chain;
   See the lorn Muse to Britain's sainted plain
From scenes of death and uproar gladly flee!
   There wake her shatter'd chords to voice
         again,
And paint, in glowing tints of ecstasy,
The sweets of ease, the pride of conquering Liberty!

K

The wreaths of song, by Fancy's fingers twined,
From witching harmony's serener bowers,
May charm the senses and refine the mind,—
But lull and captivate its noblest powers.
And, at this time, when ruin round us lowers,
What place for syren luxury's control?
Oh, for that strain, whose bursting grandeur
showers
The fires of ardour on the listening soul,
And sweeps the raptured wish to glory's arduous
goal!

Ye scenes of Peace, ye gentler themes, adieu!
The last, the weakest of the minstrel throng
Withdraws his fond, regretful thoughts from
you,
And proudly bold would dare a nobler song;
Would suit his numbers to the cadence strong
Of sulphurous thunder, and, on feet of flame,

Through groans and slaughter shuddering along,
Would leave his nature-pointed path to fame,
To earn his dearer wish, to earn a Patriot's name!

Thrice happy could his artless descant light
   A ray of spirit through his native land,
Redeem one bosom from despondence' night,
   Or rouse to rivalry one slumb'ring hand;
   Assist the warrior's laurels to withstand,
In song embalm'd, oblivion's dull decay;
   The praise of generous purpose but command;
Oh! dare he hope so boldly for his lay,
His dread of censure's fang such hopes would far
      outweigh.

Come then, my wild, enthusiastic shell,
   Pursue thy task, conform thy trembling string,
For Gratitude claims all thy soul to swell
   The laud of them who gave thee ease to sing!

Who dash'd the Vulture Fury fain to spring
On Freedom's fair asylum for its prey !
Come then, my shell, and bid their actions ring
Their panegyric in descriptive lay—
Lo, thy transcendent theme, proud Salamanca's day !

THE BATTLE OF SALAMANCA.

I.

'Twas Summer's dawn, that silent hour
When night from lawn and woodland bow'r
    Withdrew her sable shroud ;
And morning up the eastern sky
Arose, with placid majesty,
    In car of silver cloud.
Old Salamanca's few tall spires
Flash'd through the mists like living fires,
And Tormes roll'd his fruitful tide,
A sheet of wavy gold beside.
Thence o'er the landscape scatter'd wild,
The citron's silken tresses smiled

In morning's mellow hue;
And here and there the leaves among
The yellow fruitage gaily hung,
    In wreath of diamond dew.

II.

Along that fair and fertile green
A brave and hardy host were seen
    To rest the weary head;
Spain, Portugal, in long array,
'Mongst Britain's friendly squadrons lay,
    All on their grassy bed.
Nor yet the infant beams, that play'd
    O'er cheeks with rosy vigour crown'd,
Had melted sleep's refreshing shade,
    Which toil had deepen'd round:
But still the dreams of morning stole
From camps and cares the warrior's soul,
Through milder, sweeter scenes to stray,

And taste of pleasures far away.
And now his footsteps lightly roam
To his neat farm and cottage home ;
And now he meets each well-known face,
And, flying to his glad embrace,
His weeping wife, his children dear,
And all his bosom friends, appear !—
Till, as he counts his labours o'er,
And vows to leave them never more!
The shrill reveillé, rattling nigh,
Scares the sweet vision in a sigh !

III.

The sentinel on foremost ground
In silence trod his lonely round,
Save when he raised his voice to tell
His answering comrade "all was well."
The scenery in its golden trim
No robe of beauty wore for him ;

His every thought, his eye, his soul,
Were tranced by duty's stern control
   The adverse heights along;
Where Gallia's legions to and fro,
That livelong morn were seen to go,
   A strange mysterious throng.
Their Chief, to wiles and battles bred,
The busy bands in person led,
   Nor skill nor labour spared;
All anxious, from the laurel crown,
Which years of hardly-earn'd renown
   Around his brows had reared;—
To-day that wither'd leaf to tear,
Which Britain's Chief had blasted there.
Exulting Marmont! could thine eye
But see the bolt prepared on high,
From that avenging hand to burst
Upon thy nation's plans accurst,
With every hope to shipwreck driven

On dark disaster's wildest wave,
Nor to thy lorn entreaty given
   E'en the sad refuge of a grave,
Wounded, pursued!—that heart of pride
With other thoughts were now supplied!

IV.

But now the Sun in godlike state
Prepares to burst his topaz gate,
   And glad th' expecting skies;
And to their various tasks around,
From grassy couch, at trumpet sound,
   The brother armies rise.
And now from Britain's mingling bands
   A troop with silent haste advance,
To where yon hoary mountain stands
   Before the Orient's bright expanse:
Yon hoary mountain wide around
   Commands the vassal field—

Haste, warriors, haste! that vantage ground
  To France must never yield!
With heart of pride, and foot of speed,
They dash the dew-drops o'er the mead;
And plant, in thought, their standard now
  On vast Arapiles's brow.

v.

Is it the rising King of day,
That shoots his beams, in bright array,
Thro' the blue mists, whose wreaths invest,
With airy coif, the mountain's crest?
But lo! a standard now is spied,
And now a burnish'd helm descried—
  Till, from the hoary veil,
A phalanx of the flower of France
Along the glittering heights advance,
With waving banner, sword, and gun,
Bright with the newly-risen sun,

And fifty men for every one
   That marches o'er the dale!—
The Britons gaze, surprised, deprest,
  And slowly file across the plain,
Upon the neighbouring mountain's breast
   To rest their weary train:
Revolving as they onward move,
  Should battle wake the trump to-day,
  How advantageous through the fray
Still to the Gauls that hill must prove,
That rear'd his giant brow on high,
The arbiter of Victory!
And many a sigh of honest pride
  From manly bosom found its way;
And gloomy thought was dash'd aside
   With scorn to feel dismay:
For, though a transitory smile,
Now Fortune deigns upon the wile

Of Gaul's exulting bands,
Can any bosom own despair
When Britain's sons the combat share,
And Wellington commands?—

VI.

Great Wellington! thy thought inspires
My soul with more than wonted fires,
And bids me twine with daring aim
A wreath round Conquest's darling name.
Oh, that my weak, presumptuous hand
Could wake the lyre with seraph's art!
Oh, that my wishes could command
A verse as fervent as my heart!
So might I suit my humble lay
To the high hymns that nations pay;
The first to Heaven, the next to Thee,
Victorious Priest of Liberty!

From warring India's eastern clime
Thy Sun of Glory rose sublime,
Sweeping their sable hosts away,
Like night before the bursting day:
And now its bright, meridian rays
   O'er faint Iberia fall;
Confusion to the eagle gaze
   Of devastating Gaul:
On Vimiera's trophied field
Europe's proud victors learnt to yield;
And Talavera's echoes peal'd
  The knell of France's dying fame!
O'er Torres Vedras' mountain maze,
Where Heaven and Britain join'd to raise
The ember sparks of Freedom's blaze,
   Thy sword was seen to flame;
Like that celestial scymitar,
Whose fiery terrors flash'd afar,

From Eden's hallow'd porch to chase
The afflicters of the human race!

VII.

Oh, mighty Victor, when the Muse
  Would trace thy bounty-beaming flight,
Her feeble wings the task refuse,
  Nor dare to soar so proud a height;
But thus, in admiration's fire,
She warbles with prophetic lyre;—
While Lusian bosom shall inherit
One glimmering of that noble spirit,
Which Britain gave from Freedom's shrine,
Prompter of deeds and thoughts divine;
While'er in lofty, injured Spain
A hate of treachery shall reign,
A hate of each disgrace and woe
That French Oppression bade her know;—

The fairest chaplet of applause
　From Gratitude's warm hand shall smile,
For him who saved her dying cause,
　The Hero of the Emerald Isle!

VIII.

Yes, injured Spain, a bitter draught
Thy wrath-devoted sons have quaff'd;
And dearly paid their fathers' crimes
In sad Columbia's ravaged climes.
Behold thy plains with slaughter drench'd,
　Thy cities flaming high;
The sceptre from thy Monarch wrench'd,
　And by a sworn Ally!
He comes, his hand upon his breast,
　In token of sincerity—
But ah, he clenches 'neath his vest
　The dagger brand of treachery.
Yield, Spaniards, yield your ancient throne,

And bend before an upstart race;
This choice is yours, and this alone,
　　Destruction or disgrace.
And shall a free-born people brook
　　To reverence a minion's nod;
To tremble at a dastard's look,
　　And kiss oppression's rod?
Their maids deflower'd, their children slain,
Their shrines despoil'd by hands profane,
Their homes by brutal lords possest,
Afflictions maddening every breast,
A frenzied host—they rise,—they rise,
The fires of vengeance in their eyes,
While Heaven re-echoes to the cry
Of "glorious death or Liberty!"

IX.

But down the Pyrenean steeps
Lo, a dark host of terror sweeps,

With shouts and threat'nings dire!
Like to the desolating tide,
That awful bursts from Etna's side,
O'er field and city thund'ring wide
    In cataracts of fire.
With flame and gun and battle brand
They rush upon the fated land;—
Before them happy all and fair,
Behind them ruin and despair.
The frighted mother clasps her child,
    And seeks the desert screaming wild:
The swain foresees the storm, and flies,
And, as upon the distant rise
He turns to take one parting view,
And sigh a long and last adieu,—
Sees the loved cottage of his sires,
His fields, his vineyards wrapt in fires,
Grasps his rude arms with angry hand,
And joins his country's patriot band.

                L

That patriot band, securely strong,
With generous boldness, drive along
　　To strike one fatal blow;
But headlong rage is ill array'd
'Gainst prudence, strength, and ambuscade;
Repulsed, deluded, and betray'd,
　　They melt before the foe.

X.

And now the woes of war assume
A wider range, a darker doom,
While havoc palls in funeral gloom
　　The whole tumultuous scene:
From sea to sea the midnight air
Wafts the wild burthen of despair,
The murderer's threat, the victim's prayer,
　　And groan and curse between.
'Twould seem as if the infernal band,
Rising at wrathful Heaven's command,

On this lost realm their fury hurl'd,
To raze her image from the world!
And must she sink in all her pride,
    Unpitied, unreprieved?
Will all the world forsake her side?
    Forsake her, thus aggrieved?
No, wretched land, though all should fly,
Though all should slight thy suppliant cry,
Though all a Tyrant's rage should fear,
There is one spot to mercy dear,
That never spurn'd the plaint of woe,
(No, not from e'en her fiercest foe,)
'Tis Britain bids thee yet be free,
And opes her generous heart to thee!

XI.

See o'er the deep, in solemn pride,
The gallant fleet of England glide
    Before the whispering wind!

While Ocean lifts his glassy wave,
To catch the image of the brave,
 As, o'er the prow reclined,
With wistful ken he seeks afar
The theatre of future war;
And, fired with dreams of trophies proud,
Calls lingering Eurus from his cloud.—
Blow, breezes, blow; a thousand eyes
 O'er the green surge are sent to see
The British red cross in the skies,
 And hail the friends of Liberty.
Blow, breezes, blow; in Lusia's ear
 Resounds the trump of Gallic war—
And who shall stem the foe's career,
 While Britain rides the wave afar?
The breeze blows strong; the port they reach;
Glad shouts and clarions to the beach
 Their long-wish'd presence greet;
A thousand banners rise in air,

And all with frantic joy prepare
   The foe's approach to meet:
Onward, as lions to their prey,
They rush, and Wellesley leads the way!

XII.

Now might my glowing numbers tell,
How Gaul's red spear submissive fell
   Before Britannia's might;
When proudly on the wings of fame
Rose Wellington's victorious name
   From Vimiera's fight!
How on Corunna's hill of death
The Victor spent his dying breath
   In Victory's wild huzza!
And downcast warriors, leaning near,
Breathed low a shuddering groan to hear,
The clod resound upon the bier,
   Where Moore untimely lay!

On Talavera's stubborn field
How Gaul's o'erwhelming armies reel'd,
While trumpets rang, and cannons peal'd,
    That Wellesley ruled the day!
How Lusitania's drooping sword
Was taught by dauntless Beresford
To seek the freedom she deplored
    Through Albuera's fray!
Nor, Græme, shouldst thou unsung remain,
Who swept Barossa's trembling plain,
And set in Fame's proud galaxy
A star whose lustre ne'er shall die!

XIII.

Then might I praise triumphant Hill,
    And thousand arms renown'd in fight;
Whose very names my page would fill
    With one long blaze of glorious light.
And tell how Britain's lions sprung

To meet the battle's tempest shock;
And Gallia's frantic fury flung,
   Indignant, from Busaco's rock!
How o'er Rodrigo's midnight lines,
   Through ambush'd foes, and bursting mines,
     The fearless soldier flew!
How from Badajoz' haughty tower
   His hand, in one terrific hour,
     The Gallic standard threw!
These and a thousand themes, that well
Might challenge rapture's noblest shell,
     Await the daring lyre,
Whose feeble powers would fain relate,
In numbers boldly adequate,
     Britannia's deeds of fire;
Till, 'mid a rescued nation's praise,
   To Salamanca's field she came,
To crown with victory's brightest bays
   A course of mercy and of fame!——

XIV.

And lo! in many a rainbow hue,
The Sun has tinged the morning dew
　　Along that lovely plain;
Where deep in wide and clotted streams
Of carnage he shall bathe his beams
　　Before he sets again.
Where many a wounded Frenchman soon
Shall plain his sufferings to the moon
　　Throughout the livelong night;
And many a Briton's closing eye,
Fix'd in mute anguish on the sky,
Shall ask the boon of those who die
　　Aiding the wrong'd in fight.
Yes, thousands, thousands soon must lie
　　Along that fatal plain:
Thousands, for whom affection's sigh
　　Shall oft be heaved in vain.

Just Heaven! and must the gloomy grave
   So many opening blossoms blight?
So many parents, widows rave,
   And orphans howl their hungry plight,
All by the dark, unholy plan
   Of one ambitious, bloody man?

XV.

And shall he feel no Tyrant's fears?
   Shall no remorse his bosom chill?
He that has drench'd the world with tears,
   Shall he be tearless still?
Still shall his hand, with slaughter red,
   The fiery sword of havoc wave?
And every region 'neath his tread
   Become its people's grave?
No, thunderbolt of angry Heaven,
   Thy mission now has ended late—
Thy deathful course is nearly driven
   Up to its goal of fate.

E'en now the storm begins to frown,
   Whose gathering terrors soon shall drown,
In clouds of ruin dark and wide,
   The Heaven of thy triumphant pride!
The arm, whose temper'd might represt
   Thy proudest champion's wild career;
Tore glory's chaplet from his crest,
   And broke his baffled spear;
That arm of valour soon shall roll
   Thy second minion's vaunts away—
And brand on every Gallic soul
   The deeds of Salamanca's day!

XVI.

On yonder plain the Hero stands
Amid his bright and busy bands,
And, fix'd in meditative trance,
Watches the battle-cloud of France
That on the heights, from post to post,
   Wavers, a wide, uncertain host—

Wavers, as if in doubt, where first
The flaming bolt of death shall burst
　　In thunders o'er the plain.
Now onward press the centre ranks,
Sudden they halt—when, lo! the flanks
　　　Advance—then wheel again.
As, when the Earthquake's terror-peal
　Through Nature's bosom rolls profound,
The plains in billowy tumult reel,
　The mountains bow their heads around.
The frighted wretches of the land
In silent awe expecting stand,
Till the wild region, opening wide,
Shall gulph them in its fiery tide!
Thus dark and dreadful moves the foe,
While Britain marks him from below—
　But nought her lion-heart appals:
Still ready to repel the blow,
　　　When or where'er it falls.

XVII.

Yet seems not mazed in mystery
  To Wellington their troubled line;
One ray of his sagacious eye
    Illumes their whole design.
In vain, with aimless, flickering course,
  Still ebbs and flows the tide of fight!
He well foresees its headlong force
    Shall pour upon his right.
With cautious skill he straight commands
His choicest chiefs, his bravest bands,
  There to condense their barrier line.
" Red arm in battle, valiant Cole,
Be thine the torrent to control,
    The post of danger thine.
Through Tormes' waters, Pakenham, speed—
Spur, D'Urban, Lusitania's steed,
And watch, from yonder flanking post,
The movements of their mountain host.

Be firm—be cool—remember still,
That oft the arm of prudent skill
   Retires to strike a deeper blow.
I know that Nature ne'er represt
   The fires that light a Briton's breast
      With much of caution's snow—
But why offend your conscious pride
With precepts which you all have tried,
And lodestars found to fame of yore?
Only be Britons, as before;
And Victory's flag shall never wave
But in your hand, or on your grave."

XVIII.

The clock, that peals with hourly chime
The death-bell of departed Time,
Rung out from Salamanca's tower
The second from the mid-day hour;
When, on the right, from hostile guns,

Hark ! the loud knell of battle tolls !
From hill to hill the thunder runs,
   And deepens as it rolls.
Down o'er the valley floating wide,
   Dark clouds of smoke successive move ;
And now they climb the mountain's side,
   Where Albion's red cross waves above.
Till, o'er men, arms, and banners bright,
And every object on the right,
The sulphury wave rolls black and thick ;
   Nought seen within its murky womb,
Save where the cannon flashes quick
   Its dark-red light'ning through the gloom.
Above, the ministers of fate,
   Amid the vapours winding slow,
Mark, as they sail in dusky state,
   Their victims on the plains below.
A sudden west-wind sweeps the glen—
   The volumed clouds are gone—

Lo, a long host of Gallic men
    Advancing briskly on!
Whose line within its iron embrace
Folds half the adverse mountain's base;
    While Britain on the crown
Moves on her ranks to meet the foe,
With sword advanced and bayonet low,
    Eager to hurl him down.

XIX.

Now through the village fast they fling
  That 'neath the British station lies,
When, hark! from front, and rear, and
    wing
  The scatter'd death-shower flies.
They start—they gaze—no foe appears—
Yet still the death-shot frights their ears,
    And still they fall around—

As some lone man, who walks in haste
At nightfall, through the woodland waste,
Hears something rustling in the trees,
    And, shuddering from the sound,
In every shaking bramble sees
The prowler of the forest ground.

So curb'd the Gaul his proud career,
And look'd and trod with cautious fear,
As if at each advance his feet
A bloody grave were sure to meet.—
Great Wellington from high survey'd
    This bold, unequal fray;
He joy'd to see his ambuscade
Fill their proud squadrons with dismay:
Yet, as the tide's repeated shock
At length o'erwhelms th' opposing rock,
And thousands round his warriors grew,
He trembled for his gallant few:

XX.

And " fly where " Pakenham's heroes wait
   " Upon the right," he cried ;
" Tell him to grasp the sword of fate,
   And crush their rising pride—
Oh! righteous Heaven! to Thee we trust
   The cause of this eventful day ;
'Tis Thine to shield and aid the just,
   And hurl th' oppressor to dismay!
Thine eye hath seen this nation's woes,
Hath seen the treachery of our foes—
Avert the hastening doom of Spain,
And light our arms to joy again!
Leith, Cotton, fly the van to head,
Bradford and Cole, away ! away !
At length my anxious prayer is sped,
Glory or death is ours to-day."
While yet he speaks, upon the right,
Ascends the awful storm of fight ;

M

The shout, the clash, the trump, the gun,
At once their listening senses stun :
A hill, whose bulwark rose between,
Conceal'd the battle's murderous scene ;
      But each succeeding blast
That rose on Britain's anxious ear,
Fraught with the sounds of hope and fear,
      Seem'd louder than the last.
Heard ye that shout ? 'twas Victory's
      cry !
Again ? the Gauls or Britons fly !
   And from behind the height
Now the contending hosts appear,
   The troops of France dispersed in flight,
And Pakenham thund'ring in their rear.
Oh ! 'tis a dread and dismal sight !
Leaders and armies wing'd by fright,
Weapons with carnage gleaming red,
And horsemen charging o'er the dead,

And every terror war can bear,
To crown the fulness of despair!

XXI.

Now, all around, the armied plain
Moved like a tempest-troubled main;
Where, here and there, a plume express'd
Some angry billow's foaming crest.
Rank after rank, along the field
The serried bands of Britain peal'd,

    Slow, silent, and serene;
While culverine and mortar flung
Their thunder-shower of death among,
And clouds of funeral darkness hung

    Their horrors round the scene.
High on the cliffs that topp'd the storm,
In haste, the foe was seen to form

    His long and dark array:
As the wild dogs of Zara ken

A lion rushing through the glen,
   And round their mangled prey
Gather a loud and troubled throng,
And with unreal fury long,
   To scare their foe away:
Thus, crowding round their vantage post,
With shouts and threats the Gallic host
   Assail'd the troops below;
While now up every cloud-wrapt height
Roll'd the grim tempest of their might,
   Upon the astonish'd foe!

XXII.

Nearer and nearer still they bear
   Their steely terror through the gloom;
While France redoubles her despair,
   To ward her coming doom.
Musket and cannon madly sweep
   From every hill's high crest;
But Britain still ascends the steep,

Unbroken, unrepress'd.
Each chief before his rampant band
   Strides with reverted eye,
While valour's falchion in his hand,
   Points their stern looks on high,
Where to the verges of the rock
   The Gauls in hurried wonder speed,
There hand to hand to meet the shock,
   And gaze with panic on a deed
Which little souls might well believe
Too much for mortals to achieve.
For o'er each height's redoubted head,
Firm as the rock on which they tread,
Dark as the vision of the dead,
   The British host is seen to wheel:
" Charge !" through the phalanx loudly rings,
Onward each foot with lightning springs,
Down every hand in thunder flings
   The fateful gleaming of its steel.

XXIII.

They meet—they struggle—wide around
 Bursts the dread conflict's hideous crash;
Bayonets on bayonets dash'd resound,
  Sabres on sabres clash:
A mingled tumult roars on high [1],
 The drum, the trumpet's burning breath,
The shouting victors' furious joy,
 The wounded's anguish'd shriek of death.
Has any fallen? in his stead
 Another soon, with wilder rage,
Springs o'er the dying and the dead,
 For death or vengeance to engage.
Huge is the carnage, wild the strife,
And life is bravely paid with life,

---

[1] ———— ———————— πολὺς δ' ὀρυμαγδὸς ὀρώρει.
῎Ενθα δ' ἅμ' οἰμωγή τε καὶ εὐχωλὴ πέλεν ἀνδρῶν
'Ολλύντων τε καὶ ὀλλυμένων.

          HOMER.

Fury with fury, shout with shout,
The vantage wrestling long in doubt,—
At length the British arm prevails!
　Another charge drives on amain—
The Gauls behold—their firmness fails—
　They fly confounded o'er the plain.
Onward the British battle flows,
　Gloomy and dreadful as before,
O'er columns of their slaughter'd foes,
　And arms and ensigns wash'd with
　　gore.
Each bloody grasp with bayonet steel'd,
　The fire of death in every eye,
They thunder o'er the trembling field,
　The guardian saints of Liberty!

XXIV.

High on the left a mountain rose
　In rugged grandeur o'er the fray;

Which Gallia, from her baffled foes,
 That morn had made her prey:
Vast, inaccessible, it frown'd,
The sovereign of the plains around—
Gaul's shatter'd squadrons welcomed there,
Retreat, and respite from despair.
But scarce had gasp'd a moment's breath,
When up the crags the storm of death
 Behind them madly flung:
Gaul mark'd their headlong violence,
And from her adamantine fence
 Upon her victims sprung.
Oh! Heaven! protect our breathless group!
What countless thousands on them troop,
 All hung'ring for their doom!
Fly, Britain, fly the hopeless fight!
While yet remains the choice of flight,
 Fly from thy closing tomb!
Numbers and nature, both thy foes,

'Tis weak, 'tis madness to oppose :
Thy chief himself the mandate gave,
Fly what thou durst not hope to brave!

XXV.

The British onset thus in vain
  With brightening hopes the Gauls survey,
And turn ; and form upon the plain,
  Fierce to retrieve the desperate day.
Is it the wild tornado's breath ?
Is it the thunder-crash of death ?
Or is it Britain's hosting train,
Whose rampant chargers shake the plain ?
'Tis they—'tis Cotton's hearts of flame,
That rush to tear a wreath of fame
  From hostile brows in fight !
Full on the destined foe they fall—
Where now the pride, the hopes of Gaul ?
Low on the field, blood trampled all,

Or scatter'd wide in flight!
Yet why that shriek of lorn dismay?
  No Briton ever shriek'd through fear!
Why does that anxious group delay,
  Behind the chase, lamenting here?
Alas! around a fallen chief,
In all the gloom of manly grief,
  They stand, and weep in vain!
Valour's first arm is there controll'd,
The warmest heart of honour cold,
  In brave Le Marchant slain!—
Let joyous music fill the air!
  Let pleasure light the festal dome!
Nine children and a wife prepare
  Their long-lost hero's welcome home!
But ah! that cry! and is he fled?
  Their hope, their prayer, their only stay?
Calm is his rest on glory's bed—
  But what shall comfort their dismay?

XXVI.

But hark! the din of fight
Again assails the wearied ear;
　And 'neath the fatal height,
In horrid fray the hosts appear.
The foe firm-placed and numerous stand;
　But place and numbers little daunt,
Where gleams the steel in British hand,
　　And Cole is in the front.
Breathless, impetuous, on they haste,
Where 'gainst their rashness France has
　　placed
　Her ordeal ridge of steely fire.
But vain their frenzy! still where'er
They charge, a thousand points appear,
To hush in death their mad career,
　　And dash their baffled ire.
And from the hill's impending banks
Thunder on thunder thins their ranks;

Dark, unrevenged, the weak, the brave,
　　All fill alike a bloody grave.
And must they yield? forbid it, pride!
Another charge shall first be tried.
Another charge! but scarce the sound
Woke fire and confidence around
　　Through every sinking soul,
When from the mountain's crowded head
A darker shower of death is sped,
And streams of blood are seen to spread
　　The breast of gallant Cole!

XXVII.

They see him fall—they check their speed—
Nor flight nor onset longer heed!
But, gloomy and condensed, prepare
To meet their fate with stern despair.
When on the right is heard a shout,
" Spry, bring thy squadron's fire about,

To sweep the foeman's flank, and save
The harass'd remnants of the brave."
Bless'd as the rays of dawn appear
To some night-founder'd mariner,
Rose through the rout on Britain's ear
  Thy voice, oh Beresford!
But joy's pale torch soon pass'd away—
Instead of ardour's glad huzza,
An answering cry of wild dismay
 From every tongue was heard.
They turn'd, and dark before them stood
The hero deluged in his blood!
And see that band that o'er the heath
 Bear their sad burthen, mute and slow!
And is it thou, victorious Leith,
 In all thy glory, thus laid low?
Brave patriot! though thy soul was riven
  By torture's poison fang,
Still to thy country's cause was given

Thy warmest wish, thy sharpest pang:
For now throughout the British train,
Their leader lost, their efforts vain,
A dreadful panic seem'd to reign,
  And paralyze their force ;
While hope in every Gallic soul,
  Shook from her faded fires away
  The gathering ashes of dismay,
And on sad Britain bade them roll
  Their desolating course !

XXVIII.

And, doubtless, now the trodden heath
Had quaff'd a deeper tide of death,
While France on Britain's shrinkless blade
The meed of rage in turn had paid :
Or, haply, o'er the purple plain,
  Up the steep hill of Victory,
Had paved her way with Britons slain—

For how could Briton flee?
But Wellington, who on a hill,
Ruling the wide and woeful sight,
(As one sent down by Heaven's command,
With Fate's dark fiat in his hand,)
Sublimely stood, and pour'd his will
Through the long ridges of the fight,
With heart—not flutter'd nor dismay'd,
But roused to energy, survey'd
        The storm of battle turn'd;
For as a fire, whose rising light
Grows brighter through the gloom of night,
    The Hero's spirit burn'd:
And danger's mirror only brought
The scatter'd brilliancies of thought
In one broad blaze to light his soul
The way to Glory's proudest goal!
For scarce along the battling maze
He cast one transient eagle gaze,

When to his bosom sprung
The means to succour and repel,
And " Clinton, to the rescue [1]," fell
Portentous from his tongue.

XXIX.

As when a cloud of deathful gloom,
The seaman's terror, o'er the steep
Pours its fierce whirlwinds on the deep,
Some fated vessel to entomb
Within wild ocean's womb;
So the dread voice of Wellington,
Borne through the battle's tide,
Woke their waned strength, and roll'd them
on,
To wreck the foeman's pride.
Lo! through the field, a radiant band,

[1] " Marmion, to the rescue."—*Scott's* MARMION.

They come, they come! in every hand
The levell'd steel, in every eye
The stern resolve to win or die!
Behind their ranks the sufferers bless
A grateful refuge from distress;
The rest with new-born ardour press,
   By brave example, on the foe,—
The foe that now with alter'd eye
See the grim ruin driving nigh,
And from the plain and mountain fly
      In panic from the blow.
High on their flight the British train,
Shouting and slaughtering, rush amain—
While the broad sun, that now has driven
His chariot to the verge of Heaven,
Shooting his horizontal beams
Through smoke, and arms, and ensigns, seems
In each reverted eye to flare
An angry look of red despair.

N

XXX.

Oh! for that voice, whose dread command
Ordain'd the fiery King to stand
   O'er Gibeon's holy hill;
Till Heaven's bright sword had amply sped
Its terrors on the impious head,
   And vengeance had her fill!
For as he wanders to repose
  Behind yon western mountain's head,
And even's crimson curtains close
   Around his golden bed;
High on the left, to dare their doom,
Like spirits from the nightly tomb,
   The Gauls their lines repair;
And all the scatter'd clouds of fight,
That, erst were drifted from the right,
   Collect their terrors there.
But soon that cloud again shall reel,
Before the storm of Britain's steel—

Lo! from the chase they proudly turn!
And eager to the station peal,
   Where danger and where glory burn.
A moment for their flurried breath—
   A moment for their loose array—
And all, with Clinton, on the heath,
   Are ready for the fray.
They shout—they charge—oh! who can stand
The lightning brunt of Britain's hand?
   Ere scarce a blade could drink
Of Gallic blood, in every part,
With hasty foot, and wilder'd heart,
   Into the night they shrink.

XXXI.

Rest, conquering Britons! every sword
Enough with slaughter has been gored.
Rest, warriors, rest! each weary foot
Enough has toil'd in proud pursuit.

N 2

A lighter band, that through the day,
Placed by their Chief apart the fray,
    Have fought in wish alone,
Now joyous, eager, fly to wrest
One bloody wreath from Gallia's crest,
    Ere yet her steps be flown.
And lo! the mighty at their head!
Great Wellington! who comes to tread
    Their utmost hopes to ground;—
Like to that pyre of heavenly light,
Which walk'd of old in Israel's sight,
To guide her hallow'd steps aright,
    When glooms and foes hung round.
And now they reach the flying train—
And now the battle roars again,
    In all its former din—
While night, around their dizzy heads,
Her darkest, dreariest mantle spreads,
    Heightening the terrors of the scene.

XXXII.

Distracted Gaul! how drear to thee
Appear'd that night of destiny,
When on thy army's broken flight
Career'd Britannia's whirlwind might!
How oft thy soldier raised in prayer
  His eye, and shivering hand, to Heaven,
When fright and faintness fetter'd there
  His feet by danger onward driven!
When 'mid the rout he cannot know
If his next man be friend or foe;
Until perchance a sudden spear,
  Deep in his bosom, sternly tells
The hand of the invader near;
Or fiery victor in his ear
  His frightful triumph yells;
Or when the steely spark, that flashes
From swords whose midway fury clashes,

Or sulphurous flame of musket, shows
A grim, blue host of angry foes,
Rushing with more than mortal might,
His last weak hopes of life to blight;

XXXIII.

Thus Gallia's routed legions bled;
And scarce one frighted soul had fled
    From that avenging night,
But darkness lent her friendly shroud,
And screen'd the remnants of the crowd
    Whose limbs had strength for flight.
Through tangled forests dark and wide,
Through rocks and rushing waves they hied,
Nor ceased till Tormes roll'd his tide
    Between them and their foes;
Who now, along the opposing banks,
Collect their slaughter-wearied ranks
    To snatch a short repose,

Till morn shall light their swords again
To humbled Gallia's trembling train.

XXXIV.

And now has beat the last dull drum,
    And the last bugle blown;
The watchful sentry, dark and dumb,
    Parades his round alone:
No sounds invade his listening ear,
    But Tormes' billow murmuring nigh,
Or when at times the night-winds bear
    From the far plain a hollow sigh.
Along that carnage-cover'd green
How sad, how awful is the scene!
How opposite to that which gleam'd
On morning's eye, when trumpets scream'd,
And ardent warriors, shouting high,
Rush'd wildly on for victory!

No shouts, no trumpets now resound,
  No warriors shine in proud array;
But broken arms are scatter'd round,
  And corses strew the bloody clay:
No voice disturbs the ear of night,
Save where the wounded groans his plight,
  From 'neath a heap of slain:
And here and there a pitying throng,
That bears some dying man along,
  Is all that walks the plain.

XXXV.

Thou, hapless Lady, thou wert there,
In all thy wildness of despair,
  Who, at the voice of rumour, fled
Upon the wings of swift delight,
To hail thy victor from the fight—
  But met his corse instead!

Distracted maid [1]! what pitying tongue
  Can speak her exquisite distress,
When o'er her slaughter'd Lord she hung,
  And call'd on Death her heart to bless?
And oh! how many a soul must bleed
  Of lover, parent, child, and wife,
In death's dark page, through tears, to read
  The names of those adored in life;
For ever lost! for ever fled!
  And none to bear their last request!
No hand to smoothe their dying bed!
  No tear to dew their turf of rest!
Ye mournful band! your wounds are deep,
  And who shall chide your plaintful sigh?
But still remember, while you weep,
  They died, as heroes love to die!

---

[1] " Infelix virgo !"—VIRGIL'S ECLOGUES.

In Honour's arms they sunk to rest;
  High ardour chased each pang away :
Their deeds shall fire the soldier's breast,
  And nerve his hand in danger's day.
Their grateful country shall enrol
  Their names on Glory's lists divine,
And God Himself shall bless the soul,
  A sacrifice from Freedom's shrine !
No widow, orphan o'er their head,
Shall wail their wrongs, or cry for
        bread :
Their wives become their country's care,
Their children find a father there.
Oh! generous Britain! round thy brow
Thy acts of mercy seem to throw
A heavenly crown, of purer flame,
Than e'en thy deeds of warlike fame !

XXXVI.

Amid the dew, beneath the sky,
   On either side the stream,
The warriors close the bloodshot eye,
   And stretch the wearied limb.
But far diverse the thoughts that roll
O'er either army's anxious soul!
Far different feelings bid them view
The Orient welkin's brightening hue!
The Gaul, by fear forbade to sleep,
Condemn'd all night to pray and weep,
Watches with trembling eye the light,
The harbinger of harass'd flight,
Sighs, for his trophies, now no more,
And thinks what ills are yet in store,
How many perils, and fatigues,
And hungry hours, and rugged leagues,
Ere his sad heart may hope to find
All that is loved and left behind.

If slumber fled the Briton's eye,
'Twas exultation bade him fly ;
If that he watch'd the coming day,
'Twas but to chide its long delay ;
If homeward stray'd his joyous thought,
  It stray'd some evening hour to hail,
When, round the faggot, in his cot,
  The swains should wonder at his tale,
His tale with vaunts and conquests rife,
On march, in quarters, and in strife.

XXXVII.

If such the thoughts that then possest
  Britannia's meanest son,
What feelings must have fired thy breast,
  Triumphant Wellington ?
While the world's anxious eye was cast,
  With many a trembling wish on Thee,
To see thy proudest hopes surpass'd,

By this bright day of Victory!
To see a Chief and veteran band,
  (Who boasted in their pride
  From Victory's very side
To have received with eager hand
Her keenest, strongest brand of doom)
  With all the laurel trophies crown'd
Their hands had glean'd from nations round,—
  A mighty sacrifice to come;
And yield reluctant all their bays,
To heap the altar of thy praise!
High gifted man! whoe'er survey
The actions of that glorious day,
See hosts so oft in danger tried,
With place and number on their side,
Spite of each vantage, yielding still
To Britain's fire and Wellesley's skill,
Or friend or foeman must declare,
The hand of Fortune sway'd not there!

No, mighty Chief, relenting Heaven
To thee a glorious task hath given ;
Hath steel'd thy arm, illumed thy mind,
And bade thee succour lost mankind ;
With thee the signal spear hath hurl'd,
To crush the Tyrant of the world.
Hark! how the nations round proclaim
The praises of thy deathless name,
      And hymn thy battles won!
And Britain, bounding 'midst her tide,
Takes up the strain, and spreads it wide,
To tell the listening world, with pride,
      The greatness of her Wellington !

CONCLUSION.

THE song is hush'd—the vision'd pomps of fight
  Sink from my eye, and die upon my ear!
Lost is the shout of wrath, the cry of fright;
  Arms, flags, and battling hosts no more ap-
    pear.
  But loud upon the gale I seem to hear
The voice of triumph from another shore!
  On Britain's isle ascends the gladsome cheer.
Awake, my shell, thy failing chords once more,
Join in the festal hymn, and all thy task is o'er.

First, unto Thee, benignant Heaven, we pay
  The sacred anthems of our grateful pride!
Whose mighty hand on this auspicious day
  Hath borne the sword of vengeance on our
    side :

How shall our words express the votive tide
Read in our swelling breasts our thoughts of
　　flame!
Oh be thy dread assistance still supplied
To Britain's arm, to Britain's generous aim,
And whet her hallow'd spear the men of blood to
　　tame.

And next, O Wellington, to thee is due
　　The plausive tribute, and the laurel crown!
And them with thee, whose kindred spirits flew
　　For Britain's safety to despise their own!
　　Hail to the gallant sons of pure renown!
　　Hail to the guardians of their native strand!
　　　Oh! gracious Heaven, around their head hang
　　　　down
Thy sacred mantle—speed their generous hand
To blast oppression's plans, and save an injured
　　land!

Flush'd with success, we saw the lawless crowd,
    (Whose every threat the nations wont to weep,
As deed already done)—they rush'd—they vow'd
    To whelm our slighted legions in the deep.
Oh feeble boast! from Torres Vedras' steep
    Behold the furious bloodhounds kept at bay!
Behold them fly from thence, a troubled heap,
    Distress and danger lowering round their way,
Till their last hopes are quench'd in Salamanca's
    fray!

Rise, Spaniards, rise, and grasp the battle brand,
    Avenge your wrongs,—redeem your trampled
    laws;
Rise, and repel the harpies of your land!
    For now the foe his iron rod withdraws;
And to sustain his brethren's baffled cause,
Calls off his hordes, and leaves you time to
    dare,—

o

Curse on the wretch who slights this happy
pause,
To rush in arms to Freedom's shrine, and
swear
His dying land to save, or her sad fate to share!

They wake—they rise—they cast their bonds
away,
Burst the vain fetters of their erring pride;
'Neath Britain's standard join in firm array,
And call on Wellington their rage to guide!
Lo to thy doom, proud Tyrant, far and wide
The precepts of the British Fabius fly!
Hear'st thou the shouts that on the north
wind ride?
Hear'st thou, dark man, thy hapless people's
cry,
To sink 'mid Russian snows, and curse thee as they
die?

Behold the murderers of the world's repose
 Advance in mad ambition's full career;
The summer sun upon the pageant glows,
 And visionary spoils their labours cheer,—
 But famine and disaster hover near,
And midst the waste spring down upon their prey.
 Ruin and dearth instead of spoils appear—
Repulsed, distress'd, beset upon their way,
Thousands on thousands fall in horrible dismay.

When, righteous Heaven, will all these horrors
 cease?
 When will the measure of thy wrath be
  spann'd?
When will thy angel ministers of peace
 Descend on earth, and wave their hallow'd
  wand?
 Then shall the smiling muse with raptured
  hand,

Tear from her patriot lyre the sanguine string,
  And cowering to her long-loved Fairy land,
Strive on the golden links of peace to fling
A wreath of votive flowers, fresh cull'd from Fancy's
    spring.

Dublin, 1812.

TO A FIELD-FLOWER,

Found beside a favourite arbour early in Spring.

HAIL, lovely harbinger of Spring!
　Hail, little, modest Flower!
Fann'd by the tempest's icy wing,
　Dash'd by the hoary shower.
Thy balmy breath, thy soften'd bloom
　Was ever welcome here;
But at this hour of Wintry gloom
　Thy smile is doubly dear.

The storm that o'er thy mossy bed,
　Subdues the towering tree,
Flies harmless o'er thy shelter'd head,
　And wears no scowl for thee;—

But resting in security,
    Thou teachest haughty souls
The blessings of òbscurity,
    Where ruin's whirlwind rolls.

The tulip flaunts in rich array ;
    The rose is passing sweet ;—
But, ah ! with Summer's golden day,
    Their gaudy charms retreat :
But while the lingering Winter lowers,
    And saddens all the green,
Thou, herald mild of brighter hours,
    Thy soothing smiles are seen.

Thy gems are strew'd in every place,
    On every bank they fling
An early wreath, with artless grace
    Around the brows of Spring ;

In woodland wilds, in gardens gay,
  In vale, on mountain drear;
The first to meet the sunny ray,
  And hail the waking year.

Oh! thou art Nature's fondest care,
  The foster-child of Spring!
The virgin twines thee in her hair
  To dance at village ring.
The bee, in thy soft bosom, stays—
  His winglet's wild career;
The lark his morning song of praise
  Pours in thy dewy ear!

Dear, little, timorous, gentle flower,
  Sweet pilgrim of the storm,
Still, still beneath my sheltering bower
  Recline thy paly form!

No plundering grasp, no heedless bruise,
Shall harm one bud of thine:
And gaudier sweets while others choose,
The Primrose shall be mine.

Ballow-Water, April 27, 1812.

SONG.

SWEETEST daughter of the year,
Smiling June, I hail thee here.
Hail thee with thy skies of blue,
Days of sunshine, nights of dew.
Hail thee with thy songs and flowers,
Balmy air, and leafy bowers,
Bright and fragrant, fresh and clear,
Smiling June, I hail thee here.

Yet, sweet June, it is not these
Perfumed gales and whispering trees,
Blossoms shed with liberal hand,
Like a star-shower o'er the land,

Waves at rest and woods in tune ;
'Tis not these, delicious June,
Gives thee such a charm for me,
Moves me thus to welcome thee.

'Tis that Agnes on thy skies
Open'd first her brighter eyes ;
That the flower of all thy flowers
Woke to life within thy bowers ;
Gave thy charms a higher tone,
Lent thee honours not thy own ;
And for this, thy brightest boon,
Take thy tribute, lovely June.

1816.

MAY FLOWERS.

Sweet Babes, dress'd out in flowers of May,
And fair and innocent as they;
A lovely type in them we see
Of what you are, and what must be.—
Like them you rise, like them you bloom,
Like them you hasten to the tomb.—
Ye human flowers, smile on, smile on!
Your hours of bliss will soon be gone.

Soon manhood with its cares and crimes
Shall cloud these early sunny times,
And call you from your sports and flowers
To passions and pursuits like our's.

And what are all that men pursue
But flowrets, gather'd flowrets, too?
Howe'er they tempt, howe'er they please,
More fleeting and less fair than these.

Enjoyments, honours, talents, sway,
Wealth, beauty, all must pass away;
A cloud must come across their sky,
A frost but nips them, and they die.—
One flower alone, when all are gone,
Shall bloom for aye unfading on—
'Tis Grace—the treasure seek and prize;
It grows to Glory in the skies.

1817.

A. M. M. L.

A FEW brief moons the Babe who slumbers here
Smiled on her parents, and that innocent smile
Was daylight to their eyes. They thought her fair,
And gentle, and intelligent, and dared
To lean their hearts upon her. There are ways
And looks of hers that long will dwell with them,
And there are bright anticipations held,
How fondly and feelingly resign'd!
Her very helplessness endear'd her to them,
And made her more their own.—But this is done;—
The wintry wind pass'd o'er the opening flower,
And nipp'd it in the bud—and it is gone.

Still there is comfort left. It still is joy
That they can lift their weeping eyes to Heaven,

And think that one of theirs is settled there;
Can know, beyond the shadow of a doubt,
That she is safe with Him who bears the lambs
Within His bosom, and, no longer Babe
But Angel, now beholds her Father's face,
And shares the fulness of eternal joy.

Sweet Spirit, since now the ministry of love
From God to erring man is thine, O draw
The souls of those who loved thee to the place
Where thou art gone before them; make them feel
That earth is not their home; O fix their thoughts
On Heaven, on Him who once on earth took up
Babes such as thou, and blessed them, and bade all
Who look'd for Heaven become like Babes,—like
　　　　thee,
Pure, innocent, lowly, loving, and new-born.

SERMONS.

SERMON I.[1]

Ephes. ii. 12.
" Without God in the world."

In every part of the universe with which we are acquainted, God has left abundant evidence of His presence and agency; and all that we behold, and all that we experience, present us with lessons of Divine wisdom. *The invisible things of Him,* to use the Apostle's words, *from the creation of the world, are clearly seen, being understood by the things that are made, even His eternal power and Godhead.* *The heavens* and the earth, in fact, alike

---

[1] Preached in the Chapel at Saltram, October 19, 1823, and in the New Church of Lower Brixham, March 5, 1826.

declare the glory of God. From the flower that we trample under foot, to the planet that rolls in majesty above our heads, all things speak His praise; all declare that they were made by Him; and that He who made them is infinite in wisdom, power, and goodness. The dispensations of Providence speak the same language. Effects demand a cause: and the existence, order, variety, and continued support of the universe, drive us to a Superintending Power and Intelligence, and forbid us to be *without God in the world.*

In addition, however, to these outward monitors, we have likewise an inward witness, whose *still small voice* bears faithful testimony to her God and to His laws. Amid the ruins of fallen nature, Conscience still holds her place, the stern arbitress of all we say, or do, or design. *Showing,* in a certain sense, *the work of the Law written in the heart,* she *bears* her *witness; the thoughts accusing, or else ex-*

cusing, one another. She remains, as it were, the last particle of that Divine breath which was *breathed into man's nostrils* at his creation, and still gives evidence of her origin: for, however slighted, or stifled, or perverted, her testimony may be, she will not altogether cease to speak of her Author.

But, abundant as the witness may be which is thus given to God and His attributes, He has not seen good to leave us to these alone for instruction concerning Him. They indeed, as man was originally formed, might have been sufficient to lead him into all truth; but the state of the greater portion of mankind is a proof that it is lamentably otherwise *now*. The evidences derived from natural sources, though powerful corroboratives of the truth when once revealed, are yet, as the experience of six thousand years abundantly testifies, quite inadequate to its original development. They are indeed admirable *remembrancers*, both of God's presence, and of our duties towards Him; but still very insufficient *guides* in our attempts originally *to feel after Him*. Accordingly, God has not left us dependent on these natural monitors for instruction in such important matters. He has given us the Bible. On the page of revelation He has stamped a full, correct, image of Himself, His attributes, and His claims. He is there displayed, as indeed He is, *glorious in holiness, fearful in praises*, challenging alike our love and our respect. No human imagination could have conceived a character so exalted, and yet so suitable and consistent in all its parts. Every touch of the stupendous picture betrays the Divine pencil by which it has been sketched. The King of Eternity there *bows His heavens, and comes down*, and stands in all His majesty before us. From other sources He is revealed to us by hints, by inference, and deduction: here He is displayed, as it were, to our very senses,—He acts and speaks before us in His proper character. In other cases, examination is requisite in order to our obtaining an obscure idea of Him; here He presents Himself directly to our attention; He vindicates His presence with us, and defies us to overlook Him.

These, then, are the various witnesses and advocates of God with man. All around us and within us speak of Him; and, lest their language should be mistaken or disregarded, Revelation is added, the Bible is promulged; and, in this Christian land, a regular ministry is moreover appointed, to press its truths upon us, and leave us without excuse for our ignorance or neglect of God. By these a constant appeal is made in His behalf to all our better faculties and affections. They enforce His claims, by every consideration of duty and expediency, of His greatness and our dependence. They remind us that the issues of life and death are in His hands.

Let His sustaining influence be withdrawn from us for a moment, and we must perish. It is not necessary that He should exert His energies against us— let Him cease to employ them in our behalf, and we are instantly no more; let the Power that pervades, actuates, and upholds the universe withdraw, and the mighty machine immediately stops, and falls in pieces. If we gave but a single acknowledgment to each of His favours, every successive minute of our lives must be filled with His praises, because every successive minute of our lives comes to us loaded with His benefits. Yet, if we turn to inquire what are the practical effects of these considerations, how are these claims generally answered? I fear it must be acknowledged by every candid mind, that God and His concerns hold but a very inadequate place in our regards. If we do not openly slight Him and His service, yet surely a very small portion of our time, and still less of our hearts, are His; surely very few of our actions are performed with a direct reference to Him and His word. And though we may maintain a decent exterior, may avoid open transgression, and go through the ordinary offices of life with credit and decency; yet, surely, the actuating motives to all this must be allowed to be, in general, both mixed and defective: surely little is still done simply and cheerfully to God, and from a principle of love and duty. His service is, in truth, generally irksome to us; His worship a burden; and, so far from our deriving happiness from a sense of His presence, it commonly brings us only gloom and uneasiness. Religion, in fact, with most of us, seems to be incompatible with cheerfulness; and we therefore shun it and its Great Object. The heaviest afflictions too often fail to drive us effectually to His bosom. The most unhoped-for favours cannot melt down our hearts to Him. And, while all around seem in some degree to confess their God, man alone walks along forgetful of Him by whom he is never forgotten; the most favoured and the most thankless being in creation; and, though, surrounded with such appeals to his understanding and his heart, yet too often *without God in the world.*

When circumstances like these exist (and assuredly our consciences, if allowed to speak, will confirm the greater part of this plain representation) there must be a cause for them; and this cause must be found either in God and the things belonging to Him, or in ourselves. In the former, however, the defect cannot exist. The things which belong to God are worthy of our noblest faculties; they are fitted to engage and fill all the mind; they are without *length, or breadth, or height, or depth,* and alone suitable for an infinite and immortal soul to expatiate on. God, too, is a perfect character. In Him *is no darkness* nor defect *at all.* All which

the imagination can conceive, that He actually is.
Whatever of excellence we find in created things,
is but a glimmering ray reflected and borrowed
from the Supremely Excellent; and every object in
earth and heaven grows estimable only as it grows
like to Him.—The defect, then, is not in God or
His concerns. They are worthy of our highest
faculties and affections; and the reason why they
do not engage them must be sought in ourselves.
In truth, experience shows us that we are naturally
averse to Divine things; that there is in our very
constitution something that is, as it were, instinc-
tively hostile to God. If we obey Him, it is as a
hard task-master; if we worship Him, it is either
through fear, or shame, or some other inferior
motive, than through love. The defect, then, is in
the very disposition of man; and this must therefore be improved before we can expect any radical
change for the better.—Now this testimony of

experience exactly tallies with that of the Scriptures. They inform us that man *is* a fallen creature; that his faculties are impaired, and his affections depraved. *His heart* (for the defect is here,
even more than in his understanding) is described
there as *desperately wicked;* and it was for the
purpose of redeeming man from this degraded state
—of raising, refining, regenerating his soul, and
restoring him to the lost image and favour of his
God—that the Holy Spirit descended from above,
that the Saviour died, and the Gospel was preached.
—Here, then, we have the true reason that we are
in our dispositions so averse to Divine things, that
we are so insensible to all the judgments and
mercies we experience, and continue with so little
regret or remorse *without God in the world.*

It is a remarkable circumstance, that, wherever
God is represented in the Divine records as descending to converse with man, the latter is described

as dreading His presence.   In the brief sketch we
have of the terms on which man lived with his God
before the Fall, we find nothing but mutual love
and harmony between them ; but no sooner has he
broken the one easy command that was given him,
than the whole scene is changed, and God appears
an offended Judge; while man, a conscious culprit,
hides himself from His presence.   Wherever, in
the Scriptures, God and man again meet, if we
have any account of the feelings of the latter, they
are almost invariably full of terror.   Under whatever circumstances, and in whatever character,
God appears to him, the self-condemned sinner
trembles and is humbled before Him.   To pass
over more general instances, even the righteous
Job, however vehement and unsubdued before, no
sooner *sees Him* than he *has nought to answer ; he
lays his hand on his mouth, abhors himself, and
repents in dust and ashes.*   The first exclamation

of the holy Isaiah, when he *beholds in his temple* *the King, the Lord of hosts,* is, *Woe is me, for I am a man of unclean lips !* The shepherds of Bethlehem, when *the glory of the Lord shone around them,* and His angels descended to proclaim even the *glad tidings* of salvation, are represented as *sore afraid;* and our Lord's own disciples, when they see Him tread the waves of the sea, and enter into the midst of them after His resurrection, are both times *terrified at the sight of Him.* " *Depart from me, for I am a sinful man, O Lord,*" is the natural exclamation of fallen humanity.

These are proofs that at all times, and in the very best of men, there has existed a certain indefinite terror at meeting with their God. And if at the present hour we observe human nature with attention, methinks we may still discover traces of a similar feeling. For, though preternatural appearances of every kind may have ceased, have they, I would ask, yet lost their credence and influence with mankind? Whence the awe and agitation with which thousands still listen to every supernatural tale? Whence the terrific illusions with which superstition still peoples the darkness of the night? Whence the alarm which every strange sight or sound there excites with many? Why those anxieties that haunt the bed of sickness? Why those terrors that madden the hour of death? How is it that the meanest wretch who begs his bread from door to door, helpless, friendless, desolate as he may be, clings so convulsively to his present shred of existence, rather than venture into the presence of his God? It is, I would say, Conscience that condemns us; it is human nature that bears unwilling witness against itself. We fear to encounter an impartial Judge; for we too well conjecture what must be His sentence upon us. We feel ourselves to be unworthy of heaven; and we therefore prefer any state of known misery here, to that which we dread hereafter. But, ah! if the darkness of night fill persons with such apprehensions, how will they bear the darkness of the grave? If the illusions of the imagination be so awful to them now, what will the realities of another world be, when they rush upon them hereafter? If the presence of God in the character of mercy be so distressing, what shall they feel when they see Him *coming in the clouds of heaven* to judgment?—*Beloved, if our hearts condemn us, God is greater than our hearts, and knoweth all things;* and therefore the summons, *Prepare to meet thy God,* may well alarm us under our present circumstances.

Here, then, is the true secret of our aversion to God and to Divine things. *Our hearts condemn us,* as unfit for conversing with them. We are sinners, and therefore tremblers in the Divine presence.

Things that are opposite to each other cannot agree; and therefore, neither sinful man with a holy God, nor an unhallowed mind with heavenly subjects. If we were not aware of our unfitness for the favour of God, we should feel no reluctance to a translation into His presence.   He is a God of love alone to those who are holy; and death would be no object of terror to a pure being.   We suffer more, perhaps, at our entrance into life, than in our departure from it.   A single sigh might waft our spirits up above, and set us free for ever.   We should only go to mingle with the better part of our friends, enrolled with all the good and great of earth; we should *come to the city of the living God, to the innumerable company of angels, to the spirits of just men made perfect, and to Jesus the Mediator of the new covenant.*   But ah! the truth is, we feel ourselves unfit for such company, we do not desire it.   The service of angel and archangel has no

charms for us. We hear of no enjoyments in heaven akin to those we prize on earth. The blessed
there, find all their joy in pouring out the praises,
or doing the commands of God; and if such occupations are so wearisome to us for a time here,
what would they be when continued through eternity? In fact, according to the descriptions of the
Bible, the offices of true religion constitute the
chief happiness of heaven; and unless we find pleasure in these here, we cannot expect to find it in
them hereafter. Our Church acknowledges no pur-
gatory, no probationary or preparatory state, beside
the present life. *Now is the accepted time, now is
the day of salvation :* and if we pass through this
world *without God*, we must be without Him also
in the world to come.

Persons who are under the circumstances and
feelings now described, are said in the Scripture to
be *of the world*, and, as such, far from the favour of

God. The language of the Bible, indeed, on this subject, is awfully strong and expressive. *We cannot*, it says, *serve God and mammon :* but, *if we love the one, we must hate the other ;* and *if any man be the friend of the world, he is the enemy of God.* In fact, a devotedness to worldly objects has the direct effect of dethroning God in our hearts. If our time and thoughts, hands and hearts, are wholly dedicated to the world, what then remains for Him? This animating, influencing, actuating, engrossing object, what is it but our god? The Lord that made us will not be content with a secondary place in our affections; the concerns of eternity claim more than the mere refuse of our time and thoughts; and if the enjoyments and businesses of life, be they what they may, so occupy us as to shut out the great business for which we were brought into existence, we are, according to Scripture phraseology, however we may attempt to soften

Q

down or explain away the term, *of the world*, therefore, of necessity, *without God.*

Whoever, then, is in such a state as this, let him
remember, that, whatever else he may have, he is
yet *without God.* He may have wealth, honours,
amiabilities, talents, accomplishments; he may be
loved, revered, courted by men; his cup of pleasure
may be filled to the brim; his every appetite may
be fed to satiety; he may have all that earth can
furnish: but, one thing he has not—and that is,
God—and, whatever he may have beside, without
Him he is still poor. *What is a man profited, if
he gain the whole world, yet lose his own soul?*
Had we, indeed, all the goods that this world
could supply, we should feel their insufficiency to
satisfy an immortal soul: we should sit, amidst
them all, as others have done before, supreme yet
solitary. We should look inward, and be miserable,
if we had not something still beyond.—My fellow-

Christians, it is an awful thing, under any circumstances, to be *without God in the world*. But, ah! to be without Him in such a world as this generally proves—in a world so false, so fleeting, so full of wretchedness, and which, even in its fairest aspect, so soon must pass from us, or we from it!—When the storm grows loud and the clouds darken around us, where shall we flee for refuge, if we have none in heaven? In sickness, in bereavement, in adversity—and which of us is exempted from their visitations?—when foes assail, and friends forsake us; what shall we do, if we have not God to turn to? What shall we feel, with even Him added to the number of our enemies? And, yet, an enemy He must be, if He is not a friend. We may turn from the smiles of His love, but it must be to encounter the frowns of His vengeance. If we will not receive Him under the mild character of mercy, we must meet Him in His sterner attribute of justice. We may seek to drive God away from our thoughts, and refuse to notice or acknowledge Him; but the Omnipresent will still be near us in one form or another.

But, while we are discussing these topics, and are yet undecided, time travels on, with swift though silent wings, and brings us to the hour when we shall learn to form a true estimate of these matters. Picture to yourselves the situation of a man passing out of the world *without God*. Imagine him, as he feels at length earth sliding from beneath him, starting up to look over the edge of his present state of existence, and learning where he is and what are his prospects. With eyes opened, just as they are about to close for ever, he looks around, and discovers his awful situation. Conscience, too, that had long been drowned amidst the din of pleasure and the hurry of business, rising on him now, when least able to bear it, with her

still small voice swelling into thunder, bids him
hope no more. Bring him now his friends; give
him his enjoyments! Ah! what are they? his
soul sickens at the thought of them. He wants the
friendship of God; he wants a claim to the enjoyments of heaven!—Well! the struggle ends!—He
is gone!—Gone! whither? to the grave? No; *there
is no rest for the wicked*, not even the rest of the
tomb. He is gone *to meet his God;* to meet the
withering look of the Saviour whom he slighted;
who might have been his Advocate, but is now his
overwhelming Judge;—He is gone where no *rocks
will fall on him*, nor *mountains cover him* from
the face of outraged Omnipotence; he is gone to
the place *prepared*, not only for the incorrigibly
wicked, but for *all the people that forget God.*

The picture I have here drawn is a gloomy one.
It might have been desirable to relieve it with
matter of a different cast, but time will not admit

of our doing this fully at present. There is, doubtless, another state of heart and mind, very unlike to that which we have now described—a high and holy state, in which *to live is Christ, and to die is gain ;* in which God is our Father, heaven is our portion, and the things of this world are held with the slack and un-anxious grasp of one who feels that he is a *pilgrim and a stranger on earth*, and who is looking to, and longing for, his home. If, then, that which has been said here to-day may have made an impression on the heart of any present, let him not seek to obliterate it. A serious and contemplative disposition is the soil on which the seeds of every virtue may best be sown; in which they most readily take root, and from whence they give the most abundant fruit. When we are convinced of our wants and errors, half the work of reformation is accomplished; there is no want for which God does not afford an adequate supply; no error which the Gospel will not enable us to amend. Do any feel that they have to-day had a true picture of their own state; and that they have been too much *without God in the world?* What, I may ask, what but their own unwillingness or indifference, can hinder their escaping from this condition; from going direct to God, and being His for ever? Is there not *a new and living way opened* for us to Him, through a Redeemer? Is not the *blood of the Lord Jesus Christ sufficient to cleanse from all sin?* And are there not, in every page of His Gospel, invitations and welcomes to all that are disposed to come to God through Him? Has not the Holy Spirit promised *to help our infirmities,* and speed our way to glory? And will not every angel in heaven *shout for joy* over another *sinner repenting?*—Where is the want of encouragement in the Divine word, to those that are truly humbled and penitent, feeling

that they have wandered, and desirous of return?
Are not the invitations strong enough? Are not
the promises free enough? Oh, where is the ob-
stacle to their reception, if it exist not in their own
hearts? If they are willing to return, who is unwilling that they should? Is God unwilling, who
has spared them and pleaded with them so long?
Is Jesus unwilling, who has laid down His life for
their sakes? Is the Holy Spirit unwilling, who is
even now perhaps striving with them for their
souls? Oh, let not Satan, let not the world, let
not your own indolence or indifference, keep you
from God. Go to Him, like the poor Prodigal,
and tell Him you *have sinned against heaven, and
before Him,* and are *no more worthy to be called
His son.* Tell Him you have too long slighted
His judgments and abused His mercies; that you
have too long forsaken Him for a cold and cheerless
world, and preferred its service to His, its joys

to those of heaven. Tell Him that you have at last felt its worthlessness and insufficiency, and your own guilt and folly; that you "do earnestly repent, and are heartily sorry for these your misdoings;" and that you would now return, and be reconciled to Him, and dwell with Him for ever. Tell Him this in humbleness and simplicity of heart; and depend on it the Lord will not reject His child, His creature, His repenting suppliant. He will *lift up the light of His countenance on you and bless you.* And, if *He be for you, who can be against you?* If He be your friend, what good thing can long be absent from you? You will have, through Him, peace in life, hope in death: and this once passed, then *lift up your heads, O ye gates; and be ye lifted up, O ye everlasting doors; and the King* and the heirs *of glory shall come in.*

SERMON II.[1]

John xxi. 6.

" Cast the net on the right side of the ship, and ye shall find."

It was my intention, brethren, to have addressed
this congregation from a different text, and on different topics, from those which I am now about to
bring before them. But the affecting and interesting sight which presents itself here to-day, induces
me to select a subject more directly suitable to our
dear fishermen, whom I so rejoice to meet in the
House of God this morning. There is surely not
one person present who does not partake of the

[1] Addressed to the Fishermen of Brixham, on the Sunday
after the Coronation, 1838.

emotions which I feel in standing up among such a body of my parishioners, and who will not excuse me for addressing myself on this occasion almost exclusively to them. Join me then, my dear friends, in praying, that the words spoken in weakness may come in power to the hearts of those who hear, and prove *a savour of life unto life* to many among us.

The manner in which our fishermen have conducted themselves throughout this week, cannot have failed to gratify all who have witnessed it. The people of Brixham may well be proud of a body of men, who have so practically proved that they can command themselves. If, my dear friends, there has, heretofore, been any grounds for doubt on this point, your proceedings through the past week have done much to wipe off the reproach, and your own hearts must at this moment be richly enjoying the moral triumph you have achieved. It was highly gratifying to all the friends of order and sobriety in this place, to hear of the admirable determinations with which you opened your proceedings on Thursday; and it is the more encouraging to think, that these determinations arose, and have been maintained, altogether among yourselves. You were right indeed in thinking, that a man is never more degraded than when in a state of intoxication; he truly then places himself below the level of the brute, for the brute will not voluntarily deprive himself of his sober senses. The inward satisfaction which you must now enjoy in the review of the last few days, is surely more than a recompence for any self-denial that you may have imposed on yourselves; and let me hope that this experience of the past may, through God's blessing, give you moral encouragement, moral strength, for the future; and that the conduct of this week may prove the auspicious earnest, the happy first-fruits, of a rich and abundant harvest.

But if the opening of your proceedings was praiseworthy, the close of them is not less so. To meet you here, my brethren, in the House of God, to witness your orderly conduct, your devotional manner here, is, indeed, most pleasing and encouraging. It seems to me to say, that you know from whence high and holy motives and principles may alone be derived: that in order to persevere in that which is right and good, you feel that we must look for grace to Him, "*from whom all holy desires, all good counsels, and all just works do proceed.*" It seems to me to intimate, that you have a proper sense of the religious nature of the great ceremony we have just been celebrating in these realms; that you view it, as indeed it is, as a solemn national transaction, carried on in the sight of God, in one of His holy temples, between His Vicegerent on earth and the people He has committed to her charge; and that you are aware that God must be appealed to, in order that sho may

prove a blessing to us, or that we may be enabled
to discharge our duties to her. My dear friends,
nothing is really great in which God and religion
have not a place. Deprive the coronation of these,
strip the pageant of its heavenly halo, and how
poor and insignificant does it become! It is, as
connecting itself with God, with His will, His sanc-
tions, His appointment, and His blessing, that the
ceremony becomes truly impressive. In this light
I trust that your presence here to-day shows that
you view it. It is, I trust, as if you said, we have
but half discharged our duty on this occasion, till
we have gone to the house of God and asked His
blessing on our youthful Sovereign; asked the
King of kings and the Lord of lords to supply the
deficiencies of our services towards her. The
prayers, in which we have all joined here to-day,
afford a striking compendium, both to monarch and
subject, of their respective duties to each other;

and I trust that we shall all make a point of study-
ing their contents, and of pouring them forth earnestly every Sabbath at the throne of grace.   Then
may our loyalty be expected to be, not like the
vows and garlands that adorned the festal hour,
and then faded away; but like the jewels of the
royal crown, that have come down, precious and
untarnished, through successive generations.   O
let the loyalty of British hearts once thus vent
itself in fervent persevering prayer for their Sovereign, and who shall say what benefits may thus
descend upon her head, and through her upon her
people ?

Your presence, however, here to-day implies, I
trust, even something more than enlightened loyalty
to an earthly monarch ; it shows that you recognize
the superior claims of *the King eternal, immortal,
invisible, the only wise God,* on the homage and
allegiance of His creatures.   Whatever God's Re-

presentative on earth may demand from us, such demands are few and feeble, compared with those of God Himself; and the utmost that duty and devotedness can bestow may well be offered at the feet of Him, to whom we owe all, and on whom we depend for all. That great coronation-day will come at last, when, before the assembled universe, amidst ministering angels, the crown shall be placed upon the bleeding brow of the Conqueror of sin and death, and *all things* in heaven and earth *be put under His feet;* and it is the interest, as well as the duty of His servants now, to learn to enthrone Him in their hearts; to learn to *cast their crowns before Him;* to learn how to join in the universal acclamation, the *Alleluia,* the *honour, glory, power, and blessing,* that shall then burst forth from every tongue. I rejoice then to meet you here, anticipating, in the House of God, some of the holy services of Heaven. *Fear God,* and *honour the king,* are,

R

we know, coupled together in the Bible. *Render
unto Cæsar the things that are Cæsar's* is immediately followed by Render *unto God the things that
are God's.* And there is truly no office of life that can
be properly performed, till we are duly sensible of
our religious obligations, and till the motives to its
performance are drawn from the sanctuary. It is
the religious man that is always, and in every rela-
tion of life, the best member of society; the most
useful to others, and the most happy in himself:
and be assured, my dear friends, that no man ever
casts the net on the right side of the ship, none ever
catches any thing worth his finding, who does not
seek and find the favour of God through Christ,
forgiveness of sins through His blood, the hope of
glory by His merits, the preparation for Heaven by
His Holy Spirit, and all the blessed motives and
principles, which keep a man in the narrow way
through this life, and bring him to everlasting hap-

piness in the life to come. Whatever else may be sought or acquired by us, if these be neglected, we shall find at last that we have *toiled all night and caught nothing;* yea, toiled in vain through the night of time, and found nothing but disappointment for eternity.

The language of the text was addressed by our newly-risen Lord to Peter and his fellow-fishermen of Galilee; who, after the bitter disappointment they had experienced in seeing their Lord and Master, Him of whom they *had trusted, that it had been He that should have redeemed Israel,* crucified and slain, had returned to their ordinary occupations at the sea of Tiberias. Jesus had called them originally to be His disciples by a miraculous draught of fishes, and He now revived their slumbering faith and hopes by a similar miracle. He taught them His divine power and authority over all creation, intimated to them His intention of delegating a part of that power to them in making them fishers of men, and reminded them, that in order to pursue this or any other avocation with success, we must depend continually on His guidance, on His blessing. Such is the lesson which the words still convey to you, my brethren, and to me. They contain a direction and a promise applicable to all circumstances in which we may be placed; teach us, that on every occasion there is a right side of the ship for us, one to which God's word points, and in which His blessing may be expected, and that it is only when we cast in the net there that we may hope to find. This lesson of dependence is applicable to all cases and persons, but it is peculiarly so to those who *occupy their business in the great waters,* and above all to fishermen. God indeed gave man at the first *dominion over the fish of the sea,* as well as over the fowls and brutes, but how little could we do to-

wards exercising that dominion without His special
interference! Diligence and perseverance and in-
genuity, needful as they are, could effect but little
in the exercise of the fisherman's craft, unless God
was pleased to add His favour and blessing. If but
an east wind, you know, prevail for a few weeks, as
it sometimes does, on our coasts, what distress and
destitution does it bring with it to the fisherman!
How sternly does it admonish those who *sacrifice
unto their net, and burn incense unto their drag*, to
depend not on these, but on Him who *brings forth
the winds from His treasury*, who stills the waves
with a word, and overrules the restless elements to
His will and *our* good! My dear friends, He from
whom we thus derive our all, is not the Being that
we ought lightly to offend. His Sabbaths ought
not to be rashly broken, His house deserted, His
name profaned, His word neglected. A sailor's
heart is generally a warm and generous one: he

scorns to be ungrateful for, insensible of, the lightest favour; and yet he too often thinks little of
insulting and trampling on Him, to whom he owes
more than to all beside. He thinks little of irre-
verence and ingratitude towards God. O, I am
sure, that if the honest, manly hearts that are now
before me, thought a little more of their obligations
to Him; of all that He does for them and bears
from them; of the manner in which He hourly
spares and tends them; of the provision He daily
makes for them, the protection He daily affords
them; of the means He uses for awakening and
blessing them; of the mighty machinery He puts
in motion for their salvation, the gift of His dear
Son to be their Redeemer, the descent of His Holy
Spirit to prepare their souls for heaven; all the
means of grace that He provides for them; all the
hopes of glory He holds out to them; if these
things were but duly thought of, I am sure that

sailors could not blaspheme God's name as they do; could not turn their backs on His house; could not shut their ears to His invitations; could not cast contempt on His ordinances. No, they would soon throw themselves down in sorrow and shame at their Benefactor's feet; and determine, through His grace, *to worship Him, serve Him, and obey Him*, in a very different way for the future.

But not only does *gratitude* thus call you, my dear friends, to devote yourselves more fully to God, to ask yourselves *what shall we render unto the Lord for all His benefits to us, your own interests*, temporal and eternal, are alike involved in having Him for your friend. I will not dwell on the consideration, how little any can hope for prosperity with Him *who ordereth all things according to the counsel of His will* opposed to them. It is, indeed, specially enumerated as one of those sins which *brought evil from God on Jerusalem*, that the Sabbath was profaned by " carrying" and traffick-

ing in " fish" there on that day[1]; and I think it seems
to be now pretty generally acknowledged, that
those who rob God of His holy day, and employ
it in secular pursuits, find their temporal interests
but little promoted thereby. Without, however,
dwelling on these general topics, allow me to turn
to matters of more immediate and personal interest.
The dangers, temporal and spiritual, to which seamen are exposed, urge them more than any other
class of men to seek Divine protection and blessing.
Many persons seem to wish to keep out of sight the
precariousness of the sailor's life; and think it
politic to maintain, that men are as safe at sea
as on shore. Now it is not *my* maxim, nor do I
think it that of the Bible, to shut my eyes to the
truth, however ungracious it may be. I had much
rather look danger full in the face, and make what
provision I could to meet it; and to persuade you,

---

[1] Nehem. xiii. 61.

brethren, that you were not exposed to greater
perils than others, even if I could hope to do so in
the face of so many evidences to the contrary,
would be only to lull you into a fatal self-security,
and to *say peace, peace, when there was no peace.*
But I will not attempt thus to insult your common
sense, to contradict your every-day's experience.
Alas! the mourning weeds of too many around
me would be sufficient to confute me; widows,
and orphans, and childless parents, would, on every
side, rise to rebut my assertions: there is scarcely
a family here that has not some melancholy memo-
rial to testify to them of the dangers of the sea.
The insurance offices, those shrewd calculators of
the value of human life, will not, you know, insure
that of a sailor, without a large additional premium.
How many a gallant vessel have we seen leave this
port, her sails set, her colours flying, the breezes
fair, and the water smooth, her men on her deck

all joy and confidence, and the merchant on the
shore viewing, with pride, her departure, and calculating his gains from her return; and now the
mother has taken her last leave of her young
sailor son, and the weeping wife has been soothed
and dismissed with an assurance of a safe voyage
and a speedy and joyful re-union, and forth the
vessel glides, like a full-plumed swan, into the
deep. But by and by the clouds muster; the
storm descends; she heels; she fills: there is a
struggle; there is a cry; and the *wind passeth over
her, and she is gone, and the place thereof shall
know her no more.* She is gone to the bottom of
the deep, and her crew are gone to meet their
God! Ah, of how many a noble vessel is this
the history! And why do I dwell on these things?
Is it to damp and daunt the spirit and enterprize
of our gallant seamen? O no! It is to strengthen,
to confirm them: to induce them to lay in a stock

of heavenly energy, of Divine strength; to bid
them be strong in the Lord and in the power of His
might; to teach them to prepare for the worst
that can come; to be ready for whatever the Lord
may send; to be able, if death itself should call, to
reply in humble, yet holy trust, *Lord, now lettest
thou Thy servant depart in peace, for mine eyes have
seen Thy salvation!* That solemn hour, when we
shall exchange time for eternity, *must* come at last,
may come when least expected or prepared for.
A death-bed repentance, even under the most
favourable circumstances, is always a precarious
hope to cling to; even when persons die quietly
in their beds, such a support is not to be trusted
in. But how little time has the drowning sailor
even for such preparation as this! What! the
hour of shipwreck, with all its hurry and confusion,
its raging winds and roaring waves, its shrieks,
and agonies, and terrors; is this a time for making up

our account with God ?   Or suppose the sufferers not swept off at once to their fate : Oh, to think of some poor fellow lashed to the mast, or clinging to some spar or rock, from which each successive wave threatens to dislcdge him!   Oh, to imagine his feelings and reflections there!   What does he think now of the admonitions he once slighted? What would he give now for one of the opportunities he before threw away?   What is it that now appears to him the most important of all pursuits, the most valuable of all possessions?   Would that he had thought more of God, of Christ, of his soul, of his Bible.   Oh, that earnest prayer!   Oh, that agonizing cry, *Lord, have mercy upon me!*   May God hear that dying cry, that parting prayer, for perhaps they are the only ones which the suppliant has ever poured forth from his heart !

How different from this is the state of him whose soul is stayed on God, who possesses a well-founded hope of His mercy through Jesus Christ! In the hour of danger he is not obliged to look anxiously about him for a refuge. He flees at once under the shadow of Almighty wings, and is safe. He can gaze on death with composure, for the sting of death is taken away. He can encounter the terrors of the deep unshaken, for Christ is in the vessel, the vessel of his soul, and it therefore cannot perish. The storm may rage around him, but there is a still small voice which calms the storm within; and amidst the din of conflicting elements he is enabled to exclaim, *The Lord is my hope and strength, a very present help in trouble; therefore will I not fear, though the mountains be carried into the midst of the sea.* Ah, my friends, I need not tell you that a man is not less calculated to discharge the offices of this life when he has a good hope for the life to come. You have, me-thinks, only to look round on your own body for

evidence, that a sailor is not less effective and
enterprising and trustworthy, who is under the
influence of religion; and in the hour of peril who
is it that stands erect and unflinching, like Paul
amidst the agitated crew that he sailed with ? Who
but the man.that has God at his side ; whose feet
are on the everlasting hills, who is built on the rock
Christ Jesus, the sure foundation, which cannot be
moved ?

But we have been here only speaking of the
sailor's dangers at sea : his dangers on shore are not
less numerous and formidable, I mean the spiritual
dangers, which threaten shipwreck to his soul.
Temptation in every shape, perhaps, assaults sailors
more than any other class of the community : the
free, open, unsuspecting character of the seaman,
renders him peculiarly the prey of the designing ;
and when on shore, in a strange port, thrown
among the most abandoned characters, in the

streets and public-houses, without that great safe-
guard of morality, a home, without those uncon-
scious guardian angels, affectionate friends and
relatives, is it to be wondered that he should often
be warped from his heavenly course, and hurried
headlong down the *broad way that leadeth to destruction?* Deeply, alas, are these unhappy in-
fluences felt by our own poor fishermen, in their
yearly visits to Ramsgate, and the eastern coasts
of the kingdom ; and ill are the moral evils which
are incurred in these expeditions repaid by any temporal gains which they may bring into our place.
How many a fine young fellow have I seen, on
whose soul the most favourable impressions appeared to have been made, of whom the highest
hopes might have been formed, and over whom
angels seemed ready to strike their exulting harps,
and to welcome one more sinner to repentance ;
and yet one season spent, or rather misspent, there

was enough to blight all these opening promises, and to send him back to us demoralized, and besotted, and hardened; forgetful alike of duty and of decency! Believe me, my dear friends, that there is none more exposed to spiritual danger, none more constantly assailed by the world, the flesh, and the devil, than the sailor; and he must indeed guard against exposing himself to seduction, struggle hard with his own passions, yea, watch and pray, and strive in Almighty strength, if he expects at length to *have the victory.* You would think the master of a vessel very improvident who went to sea without a chart or compass to direct his course; who, when he knew himself surrounded with dangers, took no pilot on board, stationed no steady hand at the wheel or helm, and kept no look-out a-head for breakers; who, during a long voyage kept no log, made no soundings, took no observation, hoisted no sail when the breeze was favourable, and dropped no anchor when wind and tide were adverse. And yet what shall we say of him who ventures on the much more perilous voyage of life, without any similar precautions; who never calls on Christ to be his pilot, never consults the chart of His word, never uses the compass of God's Spirit, never rides at the sure anchor of hope, never lifts his sail to the prosperous breezes of God's grace, never keeps watch against the rocks and quicksands of the world, but lets his vessel drive over the deep without precaution or direction? How can such a man hope to make a successful voyage? How can he look for prosperity or safety? How can he expect to pass securely through the waves of time, and land auspiciously in the haven of eternity? It cannot be; they only who use the appointed means may expect to obtain the desired end. It is so in temporal things; it is so in spiritual. And as well might the husbandman

S

look for the fruits of the earth without working
or sowing the soil; as well might the fisherman
expect to obtain fish without using his hook or his
net, as the soul hope for spiritual growth here, or
heavenly joys hereafter, without a diligent use of
the means of grace which God has prescribed for
their attainment.

But if, my dear brethren, you feel the justice,
the reasonableness of these observations, let me
further remind you, that, as fishermen, you have
religious opportunities and advantages which other
seamen are deprived of: you have Sabbath privileges, which they are unacquainted with. You are
commonly on shore on that day, while they, in the
fulfilment of their calling, are tossing on the distant wave. The Sabbath bell tolls in vain for them;
the house of God is opened in vain for their reception; they hear not the preached Gospel; they
cannot join in public prayer and praise. But this,

dear brethren, is not your case. You, during a
great part of the year, are permitted, are invited,
to partake of all the privileges of public worship.
Our Sailors' Sunday School likewise offers to those
who cannot read the opportunity of learning to
do so; and to those who can, of having what they
read explained to them. You have many other
religious advantages also in this place, if you were
duly careful to lay hold on them ; and remember,
dear friends, that for every one of these you must
be responsible to Him who gave them to you.
I might pass on to the enumeration of other special
incentives to piety, which you possess in common
with others. When the seaman stands on his deck
at watch by night, with the starry firmament over
head and the boundless deep around him; can he
fail of falling into a meditative frame, and thinking
of Him who called all these things into being with
a word ? will not God come down to him, *walking*

on the wings of the wind? and will not thoughts
arise like those of David, *When I consider the*
Heavens, the work of Thy hands, the moon and the
stars which Thou hast made, Lord, what is man
that Thou art mindful of him, or the son of man
that Thou visitest him? What inducements and
opportunities has the seaman for solemn contemplation, for entering into his own soul, for
breathing up his silent prayers, for reflecting on
the love of God in Christ, and resolving to dedicate
himself to His service! And then again, in the
hour of danger and distress, what appeals are
made to his conscience and his heart! What
awakening providences, what perils and deliver-
ances are daily assailing him! Every rock and
quicksand around has a voice to call him to God;
every wave rolls a lesson to his feet; every breeze
bears an admonition on its wings; the loss of
every messmate says, *Be ye also ready.* Ah, I have

little doubt that many before me can, from their own experience, testify that sailors are not without their awakenings. You have, perhaps almost every one of you, at some time or other, been aroused, been convinced, been humbled. You have almost all, at the hour of peril, repented, and called on God, and formed your good resolutions for the future. Alas, that these feelings should too often prove but as the morning cloud or the early dew, that passeth away!

How loudly then do all these considerations call on us to arouse and exert ourselves, that matters may be better with us for the future! How emphatically do they all re-echo the language inscribed on the banner you have borne with you hither to-day, a banner so appropriate to a sailor's occupations and prospects, *Prepare to meet thy God!* How loudly do they warn you, whatever else you omit, not to omit *the one thing needful!* How forcibly do they admonish you, not to fear the pointed finger of man, the profane sneer of a fellow worm, more than the power of an angry God! How do they urge you to prize, to treasure up, to improve any good impressions which His Holy Spirit may make on your hearts; and to pray to Him to carry you from strength to strength! How do they encourage you, not to let *this* blessed opportunity slip; not to let these better feelings and resolves pass away; but to determine, by God's help, to persevere in the course in which you have now begun, to continue the self-restraint which you have this week so well commenced, to employ the Sabbath as you have this morning employed it, at the throne of grace, in the House of God, in the service of Christ, on the salvation of your own souls. In commencing from this day a holy, humble, pious, self-denying walk, you will not be less happy in yourselves, not be less worthy members of society;

you will not less benefit your employers, and not
less please your God. Be assured too, that in
acting thus you will find, in the end, that you
have *cast the net on the right side of the ship*, and
will have no reason to regret the result. The
drunkard, the blasphemer, the Sabbath-breaker,
the neglecter of God's ordinances and commands,
will find, at last, that he has made an awful mistake.
He will feel the force of that terrible inquiry, *What
is a man profited, if he gain the whole world, and
lose his own soul?* Ten thousand worlds were a
poor equivalent for the loss of one smile from God,
one hope for Heaven. Learn then to value these.
Begin to pursue them; and let not the instances
of pious fishermen be confined to the days when
Peter, and James, and John were called from their
nets to follow Christ, and preach His Gospel. The
same divine grace that wrought on their hearts,
and enabled them to give up all for their Saviour's

sake, is as near and as influential for you; *seek* it, my brethren, and ye *shall find* it, and with it all things else that are worth attaining.

PSALMS

Sung on the occasion when this Sermon was delivered.

PSALM XLVI.

THE Lord is our refuge, the Lord is our guide;
We smile upon danger with Him at our side:
The billows may blacken, the tempest increase,
Though earth may be shaken, His saints shall have
    peace.

A voice still and small by His people is heard,
A whisper of peace from His life-giving word.

A stream in the desèrt, a river of love,
Flows down to their hearts from the fountain above.

Be near us, Redeemer, to shield us from ill;
Speak Thou but the word, and the tempest is still.
Thy presence to cheer us, Thy arm to defend,
A worm grows Almighty with Thee for a friend!

The Lord is our helper; ye scorners, be awed!
Ye earthlings, be still, and acknowledge your God.
The proud He will humble, the lowly defend;
O happy the people with God for a friend!

PSALM CVII.

Blest be the mighty Lord!
The seas obey His will.
He called, and lo, the billows heard!
He spake, the storm was still!

Fierce was the swelling flood,
And weak and helpless I;
But God above the tempest stood
And made its rage comply.

Lord, still make bare Thy arm,
When dangers on us press.
What fears can move, what foes can harm,
With Thee at hand to bless?

My shattered bark O guide
O'er life's tempestuous sea;
And bring me safe through wind and tide
To heaven at last and Thee!

PSALM XXI.

LORD, Thy best blessings shed
On our Queen's youthful head;

Round her abide :
Teach her Thy holy will,
Shield her from every ill,
Guard, guide, and speed her still
Safe to Thy side.

Grant her, O Lord, to be
Wise, just, and good like Thee,
Blessing and blest.
With every virtue crowned,
Honoured by nations round,
Midst earthly monarchs found
Greatest and best.

Long let her people share
Here her maternal care ;
Long 'neath her smile
May every good increase,
May every evil cease,

And freedom, health, and peace
    Dance round our isle.

Under Thy mighty wings
Keep her, O King of kings!
    Answer her prayer:
Till she shall hence remove
Up to Thy courts above,
To dwell in light and love
    Evermore there.

SERMON III.[1]

2 Cor. xiii. 11.

"Finally, brethren, farewell. Be perfect, be of good comfort, be of one mind, live in peace; and the God of love and peace shall be with you."

Though very ill able to address you, my dear friends, I am unwilling to leave you without a parting word. Excuse me, if it is a short one, and impute its brevity to bodily indisposition and weakness.

I have just read to you the words of St. Paul in taking leave of his flock at Corinth. Of all the Churches founded by the Apostle, there was none that had caused him more anxiety and distress than that of the Corinthians,—there was none in

[1] Preached at Brixham, October 1, 1844.

which he had experienced so much opposition,—
there was none more full of contention and division,
—none in which crimes and inconsistencies more
abundantly prevailed. Still this very Church
seemed to be peculiarly dear to him. It was his
own prodigal child, whose wanderings he watched
with affectionate regret, and whose return he was
ready to welcome with tears and embraces. There
are no epistles so full of earnest and impassioned
feeling as those of St. Paul to the Corinthians.
And these words, which occur almost at the close of
the last of them, are highly suitable to every like
occasion, and give both ministers and people many
useful suggestions, to some of which we will now
advert.

First, then, observe St. Paul addresses the Corinthians as *brethren*, and in doing so brings himself down into the midst of his flock, and dwells
among them as one of a great family, one of many

children, whose common Father is God. Though highly favoured and exalted in being called to such an office as he filled, and ready enough, on proper occasions, to magnify that office, he was disposed in his general demeanour rather to identify himself with those among whom he ministered, to make common cause with them, to be their sympathizing brother, entering into their feelings, interested in their concerns, and imitating in this his blessed Master, who put off His glories, and put on flesh, in order that He might rejoice in the joys and grieve in the afflictions of His people. This word then, *brethren*, if duly pondered, speaks at once of condescension and kindness, and suggests to us the two qualities which, perhaps, more than any others, tend to give a minister influence with his flock. May He whose whole life on earth was one beautiful exemplification of these graces, pour more of His own humble and affectionate Spirit on us all; and then, may true religion be expected to flourish indeed on God's earth, *His priests to be clothed with righteousness, and His Saints to sing with joyfulness!* But next a word respecting the exhortation which follows. *Be perfect,* &c. Now, perfection, I need not remind you, is not the attainment of any created being. Still it is the duty of every servant of God to be pressing on to perfection, to be aiming constantly at higher spiritual attainments, to be striving after closer and closer conformity with The Supremely Perfect. To be, in fact, daily endeavouring to correct what is evil, to supply what is defective, and to rise to what is better. And though, when we have done all, we must still feel that we *are unprofitable servants,* yea, *miserable sinners,* who must fly to the cross for daily pardon and peace, we may yet hope, by the help of Divine grace, to make such advances in spiritual life as may prepare us on earth for a better *in-*

heritance in Heaven, and not leave us, at the last great trying hour, strangers to Him who alone can make a death-bed easy.

But the Apostle proceeds, *Be of good comfort*, or, as he says elsewhere, *Be strong in the Lord, and in the power of His might.* Exercise faith and dependance on the divine word and nature, and, in the midst of discouragements from within and without, still hope and hold on in the Lord. This, be assured, is not an unneedful exhortation to a thoughtful spirit in a world like this; and when the clouds darken over our heads, it is good to have the divine word to remind us that there is still sunshine above them, and to cry in our desponding ear, *Hallelujah, the Lord God Omnipotent reigneth!* How well might we, looking only to things that are seen, tremble often for the safety of God's ark amidst the tempests by which it is assailed! How often might we fear for our own shipwreck indi-

T

vidually! But there is One who says to the stormy winds and waves, *Be still*, and immediately there is calm and safety. O! for more of fervent faith and dependance on Him! What a comfort should we find it under every trial, and what a stimulus to every duty!

But the Apostle continues, *Be of one mind; live in peace;* cultivate union and affection among each other; be as the *members of one body*, feeling for each other, helping one another, making common cause against our common foe, and wasting none of those energies, all of which united are too little for the demands that duty makes on them, in mutual opposition and contention.

What importance our blessed Saviour and His Apostles attached to this precept, we may judge from the frequency of its occurrence in their various exhortations:—*Little children, love one another, follow peace with all men.* And what was our Lord's last prayer for His Church?—*that they all may be one; as Thou, Father, art in Me, and I in Thee, that they may be one in us: * * * that they may be one even as we are One, I in Them and Thou in Me, that they may be made perfect in one.*

Such value did our Lord set on mutual union and affection among His people. He deemed it absolutely essential to the well-being of His Church; and where once division and strife crept in, He ever expected to see every evil follow. Now, how far this principle is maintained among professing Christians at the present day, a very slight glance at the state of the nominally religious world around us will abundantly show. Alas! instead of union and harmony there is nothing but opposition, and strife, and discord. Instead of men cultivating mutual concord and good will, we hear nothing, on every side, but contention and recrimination. Instead of marching together, like one vast Mace-

donian phalanx, under *the Captain of our salvation,* to the great conflict against *the world, the
flesh, and the devil,* we turn our arms one against
another, and waste our time and powers in petty
party conflicts, while the enemy of souls looks
exulting on, and rejoices to see us doing his own
work for him. And all this, my brethren, is
carried on under the name of Christ, and with
the plea of zeal for His service; as if the first and
best evidence of that zeal were not a proper respect
for His own great precept of mutual love, and
charity, and forbearance!

My dear Christian brethren, these divisions, and
contentions, and schisms, this rending of the seam-
less garment of Christ into a thousand pieces, is
to every thoughtful eye big with ominous fore-
bodings, and tells us too plainly that, in despite
of all our boasted religious attainments, in spite
of the progress that may seem to have been made

of late in the circulation of scriptural knowledge, the extension of education, and the spread of the Gospel among the heathen, there is still something fearfully defective in our system—some rottenness at the core, some worm at the root of our gourd which is sure to blight and wither it in the end. And it teaches us, that among all our spiritual acquisitions there is one which too many of us have not yet made, and *that* the very one on which our Saviour sets the highest value.

Think then, my dear Christian friends, think of these things, and learn *to bear and forbear* for the sake of mutual union and concord; study Christian charity and kindness; seek to maintain *the unity of the spirit in the bond of peace;* and be willing to make some sacrifices, if sacrifices they may be felt to be, for the sake of upholding Christian consistency, and having it said of you as of the Church of old, *Behold how these Chris-*

tians love one another! And, thus the Apostle finally assures his disciples that *the God of love and peace should be with them.* While they were seeking to conform to His will, He would abundantly be present with them, and be to them *a sun and a shield, a light and a protection.* My dear Christian friends, there are, as you know, persons, who can live, and live apparently at ease, without God in the world. But they cannot so live with any just views of their true condition. They must shut their eyes to their real state. They cannot regard themselves as they are, accountable beings, possessors of immortal souls, expectants of death, and judgment, and eternity. Yes, they must shut their eyes to all the great realities of life and death, of the present and the future, before they can be at ease without God for a friend.

Do not then, I entreat you, make so fearful an experiment, but cultivate true religion as you value peace and security. Remember how *little a man is profited, if he gain the whole world and lose his own soul.* And unless *God be for us,* and with us, though all else may be ours, yet *lack we one thing,* and that, alas! the *one thing needful.*

It has been my endeavour, dear friends, for many years to press this great truth in public and private on you all. I have ever sought to press on you plain and practical piety—not to feed you with dry husks of religious controversy, not to amuse you with questionable novelties, but to urge you, one and all, to holy, humble, devotional, dutiful piety; and how can I better occupy this last address, which, for some time at least, I shall make to you, than in a like exhortation? Think then, dear brethren, of the parting address of the Apostle in the text, and let it be mine to you: be men of piety; be men of prayer; be followers of the meek and lowly Jesus.

Remember, that it is not party spirit, not head knowledge, not belonging to this or that body of religionists that will save you, but humble faith in the blood of Christ, and holy obedience to His blessed will. Be diligent attendants then on the means of grace; wait on God perseveringly in public and in private; keep the Sabbath holy; frequent the house of God; and, when you assemble here, think, at times, of your absent minister. O! prize and use, I say, the means of grace, and you will not find them empty vessels, but rich in the waters of life. Finally then, brethren, farewell. I cannot trust myself to say more; but *be perfect, be of good comfort, be of one mind, live in peace, and the God of love and peace shall be with you. Amen.*

SERMON IV.[1]

1 Cor. xi. 26.

" For as often as ye eat this bread, and drink this cup, ye do show the Lord's death till he come."

My dear friends, I am not going to preach a sermon to you; nor will you indeed expect one from me; yet, I am thankful to be allowed to address a few words to you; and, more especially to do so on an occasion like this. The Holy Communion of the body and blood of Christ is a solemn yet delightful subject to dwell on; and it is a rich and fertile one too, affording matter for much meditation, many discourses.

We shall therefore confine ourselves exclusively

[1] Preached at Lower Brixham, September 4, 1847.

to it now. It is but little that I can say on any
subject, and I would rather not distract your
thoughts from the sacred service that is before
us by the introduction of any thing foreign to it.
The Sacrament of the Lord's Supper is the
most solemn rite of the Christian Church. It
is at the same time the most comforting and
cheering. It leads us *back* to the time when the
disciples sat around their Lord on earth, and received His parting admonitions and consolations;
and it leads us *onward* to that day, when His saints
shall again sit around Him at His marriage feast in
Heaven, and hear His voice, and behold His face in
glory. In the mean time, on their journey thither,
toils and difficulties beset them; and here in this
holy feast their Lord supplies them with strength
and support against them. As the angel said to
Elijah in the wilderness, *He* says to his wayfaring
people here, Arise and eat, because the journey is

too great for thee, in thy own strength. And if we, like the prophet, eat and drink in faith and thankfulness of the food He offers us, we like him may hope to go many days in the strength of that meat. Hear how our blessed Lord Himself speaks of the efficacy of that sacred food: *My flesh is meat indeed, and My blood is drink indeed. He that eateth My flesh, and drinketh My blood, dwelleth in Me, and I in him. As the living Father hath sent Me, and I live by the Father, so he that eateth Me, even he shall live by me.* Yes, the Lord has instituted *no* ordinance in His Church that is not rich in blessings to those who rightly partake of it. He does not present a cup of His life to servants that shall mock them with emptiness. Least of all can it be supposed that His Sacraments would partake of this character; and if they are not effectual means of peace to us, full, free, copious channels, by which the streams of spiritual life may flow to our souls, the fault, depend upon it, is in ourselves, and not in them. We expect and desire little; we open not our mouths, or rather our hearts, as we ought: and can we wonder then that God does not fill them? Among the various lights in which this Holy Communion presents itself to our view, I must content myself with merely touching at present on two, both of them sufficiently obvious, but not on that account the less worthy of our consideration. It shows forth, we are told, the Lord's death. It presents us with a vivid picture of that awful event. It brings that mighty and mysterious act in the most striking manner before our very senses. The broken bread represents His body, broken and pierced upon the cross; the poured out wine exhibits His blood flowing freely for the *remission of sin.* While partaking of these hallowed emblems we can speak with the Apostle, not merely of *that which we have heard,* but *which we have seen*

with our eyes, which we have looked on, and our
hands have handled of the word of life. And we
thus vividly behold and apprehend Him in the
astonishing act of yielding up His life for our
Redemption. Now while they are in the Christian religion abundance of holy truths worthy of
our notice and consideration, (and while he who
slights or overlooks any to which God in His wisdom
demands attention, will be fearfully responsible for
such neglect,) there is still one great truth, that
rises pre-eminent above all others ; one mighty fact
that should more than all besides fill the Christian's
eye and heart—and that is, the death and sacrifice
of his Saviour. There is no fact beside so touching, so eloquent, so persuasive as this. None that
speaks so awfully of our condition by nature; a
condition that needed so stupendous a sacrifice !
None that so assures us of the sufficiency of the
remedy ; for what can be wanting where God spared

not His own Son for our ransom ?   There is nothing
so calculated to make the thoughtless pause and
tremble as to look at Jesus agonizing in his behalf;
nothing so fitted to awaken every grateful and
generous feeling in the soul, and stimulate it to
daily duty and self-denial; nothing that can bring
such comfort to the penitent, or present such a
pillow of consolation to a dying head.   O brethren,
I can speak feelingly, experimentally on this latter
point; and I stand up here among you seasonably
to-day, as alive from the dead, if I may hope to
impress it upon you, and induce you to prepare for
that solemn hour, which must come to all, by a
timely acquaintance with, appreciation of, dependence on, the death of Christ.   And if you would
realize that death to your souls, here is the sacred
ordinance which God has appointed for that purpose ; here is the blessed rite that can best bring
it home to your hearts, *As often as ye eat this*

bread, and drink this cup aright, *you* not only *show forth*, but taste and enjoy, *the Lord's death till He come.*

But we must proceed to the other point of view in which this hallowed ordinance presents itself; one perhaps of a still more inviting and attractive nature. It not only renews for us the great sacrifice of the cross, but it spreads for us a feast of love, and says to all that *hunger and thirst after righteousness, Come, eat of my bread, and drink of the wine that I have mingled.* When a sacrifice was offered up of old, it was always followed by a holy feast. The parts of the victim that remained unconsumed were eaten by those who had made the offering, and they rejoiced together in the hope that God had been appeased by it. Now in the blessed ordinance that comes this day before us all, this is beautifully maintained and preserved. We have there not only the mighty sacrifice of the death of Christ, but the feast upon sacrifice likewise.

The body and blood of the Mighty Victim are not
only offered up to God, but they are presented
likewise to us, for our spiritual food and refresh-
ment. Yes, *if with a true penitent heart and lively
faith we receive that Holy Sacrament, we spiritually
eat the flesh of Christ, and drink His blood; we
dwell in Christ, and Christ in us; we are one with
Christ, and Christ with us;* and as the bread
and wine go to nourish and sustain the outer
man, so do the body and blood, which they repre-
sent, support and strengthen the inner man of the
soul in all those who receive them as they ought.
Here then, from His holy table the Saviour still, as
of old, feeds His feeble disciples, saying, *Take, eat,
this is My body, which is given for you*—this is My
blood, which is shed for you,—the ordinance is still
the Lord's Supper as well as the Lord's sacrifice.
We hold communion in it with Him, and with each
other; and find in it, like the Israelites of old, not
only the blood of the Paschal Lamb wherewith to

sprinkle the door-posts, but food to strengthen us for the journey that is before us. It is in this point of view, as I have said, that the ordinance presents itself to us in a peculiarly attractive and alluring form. The Saviour exhibits Himself in it in His endearing and condescending attitude; inviting us to sit down and eat and drink with Him, and granting us a nearness of approach to Him: a fulness of intercourse with Him, which by no other means, and on no other occasion, can we hope on earth to experience. The death of Christ on the Cross, without this relief, would be an object of awe and distress. The contemplation of Him as He now is, in glory, would overpower us with its grandness. The prospect of His coming in the clouds of Heaven to judgment, might well overwhelm us with apprehensions. But in this beautiful and benignant ordinance He meets us as the Friend of sinners, as *the Lamb of God that taketh away the sins of the world*. As He that *gave Himself* of old *to redeem us from our iniquities*, and still gives Himself to those who meet Him at His holy table, to feed them with *the bread of life*, and refresh them with the streams of salvation.

And now, my dear friends, having presented this holy ordinance before you in these twofold points of attraction, as renewing the great sacrifice so indispensable to our pardon, and as spreading a sacrificial feast for us, rich in spiritual life and consolation, let me ask all before me, How they intend to meet its recurrence? When the Saviour hung upon the Cross at Jerusalem, those that stood around Him there were actuated by various emotions. Some *hated and reviled Him;* some tortured and slew Him; some shouted, *Crucify Him, Crucify Him.* While others, we hear, *stood afar off,* looking on, perhaps with unconcern, or holding back with cowardly selfishness from Him who then most needed their sympathies. A few, and very few, we find clinging to the foot of the Cross. His mother

and the beloved disciple, and one or two besides.
Now, which of all these, my brethren, do you intend
to imitate here to-day ? Not, I am sure, inten-
tionally, His murderers and revilers, though, be it
remembered, that there is such a thing as *crucify-
ing the Lord afresh.* Nor was it the Jews or the
Gentiles that in reality slew Him ; not the spear,
nor the nails that wounded and pierced Him, but
the sins, the sins of His creatures. Let us take
care then, lest we should come under even this
class of the spectators of Christ's Crucifixion.
But there were others, again, that *stood afar off,*
that looked on with indifference, or that turned
their backs coldly on the spectacle, as a matter in
which they had no concern. Shall we to-day imitate in our conduct and turn our backs on Him,
who *gave His life for us ?* Or shall we not rather
with the faithful few press to the foot of His
Cross, to tender Him the homage of our hearts,
and hear in return His parting benedictions and

injunctions?   On receiving the ordinance in another light, as the Supper of the Lord, may we not,
every time that it is spread before us, hear from
that table a solemn voice, the voice of the Saviour,
saying to all present, *Will ye also go away?*   A
great Supper is prepared for us, *the oxen and the
fatlings are killed, and all things are ready.*   Are
we ready to hear the invitation that is made to
us?   Or shall *we go our way, one to our farm, and
another to our merchandize,* and make light of the
feast and its Provider?   Weigh this question with
yourselves, my brethren, and the Lord direct your
decision.   For how shall they who slight His
ordinance here, hope to sit down at the great Marriage Feast above?   How shall they who reject
His invitations hope to share His promises and
blessings?

THE END.

GILBERT & RIVINGTON, Printers, St. John's Square, London.